Princesses, Unicorns, and Butterflies

MW00887883

THIS BOOK BELONGS TO:_________________

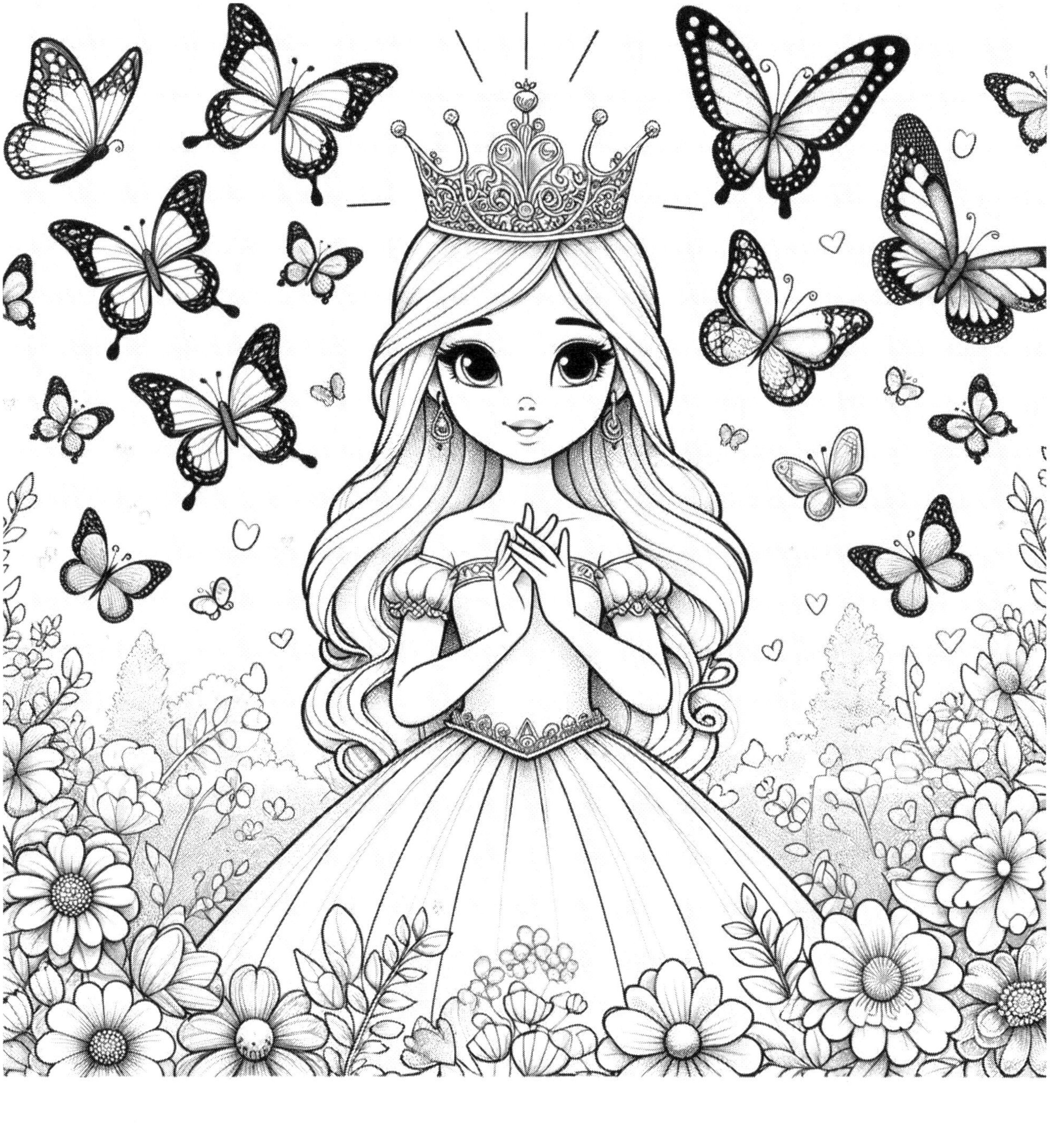

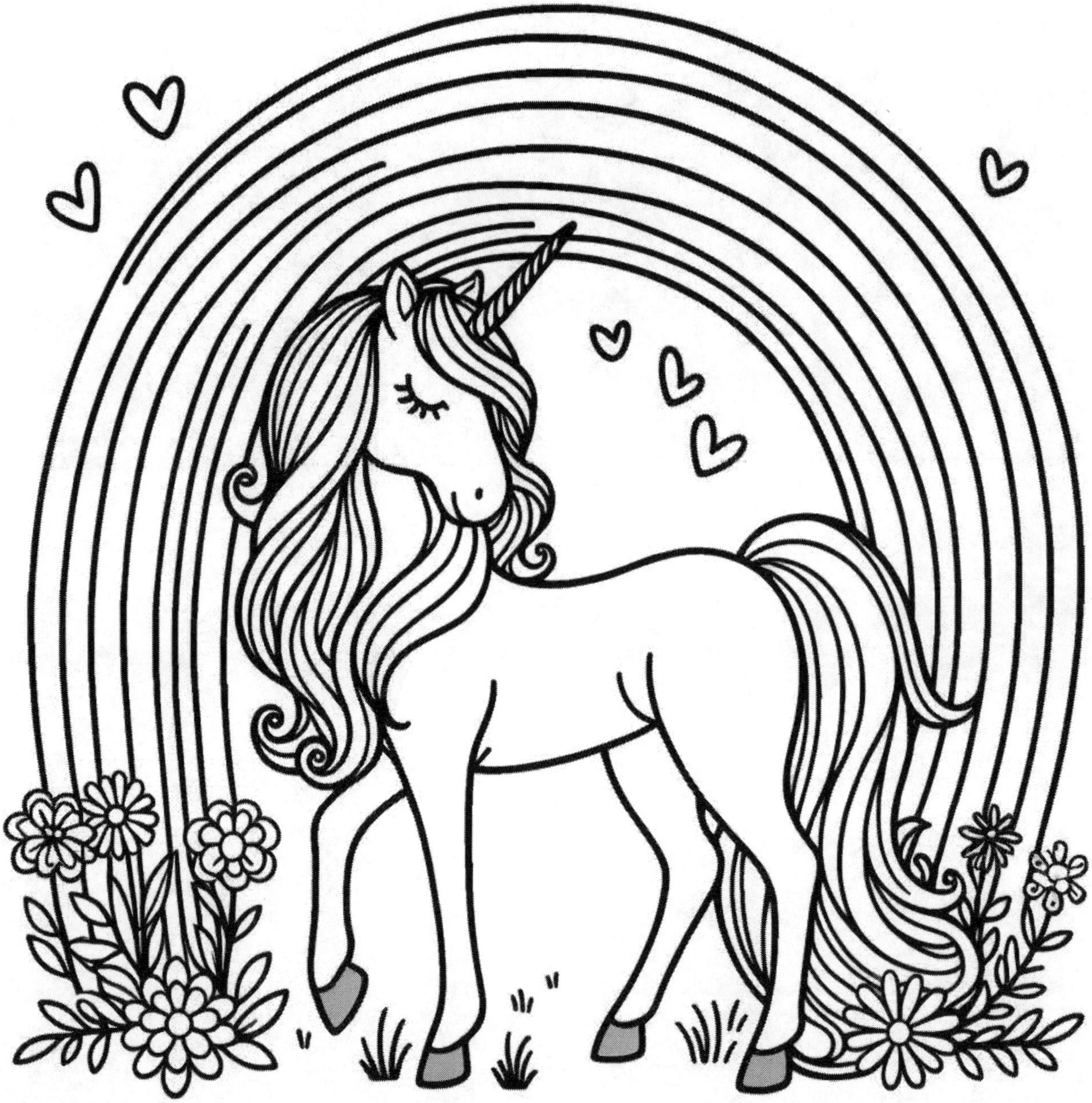

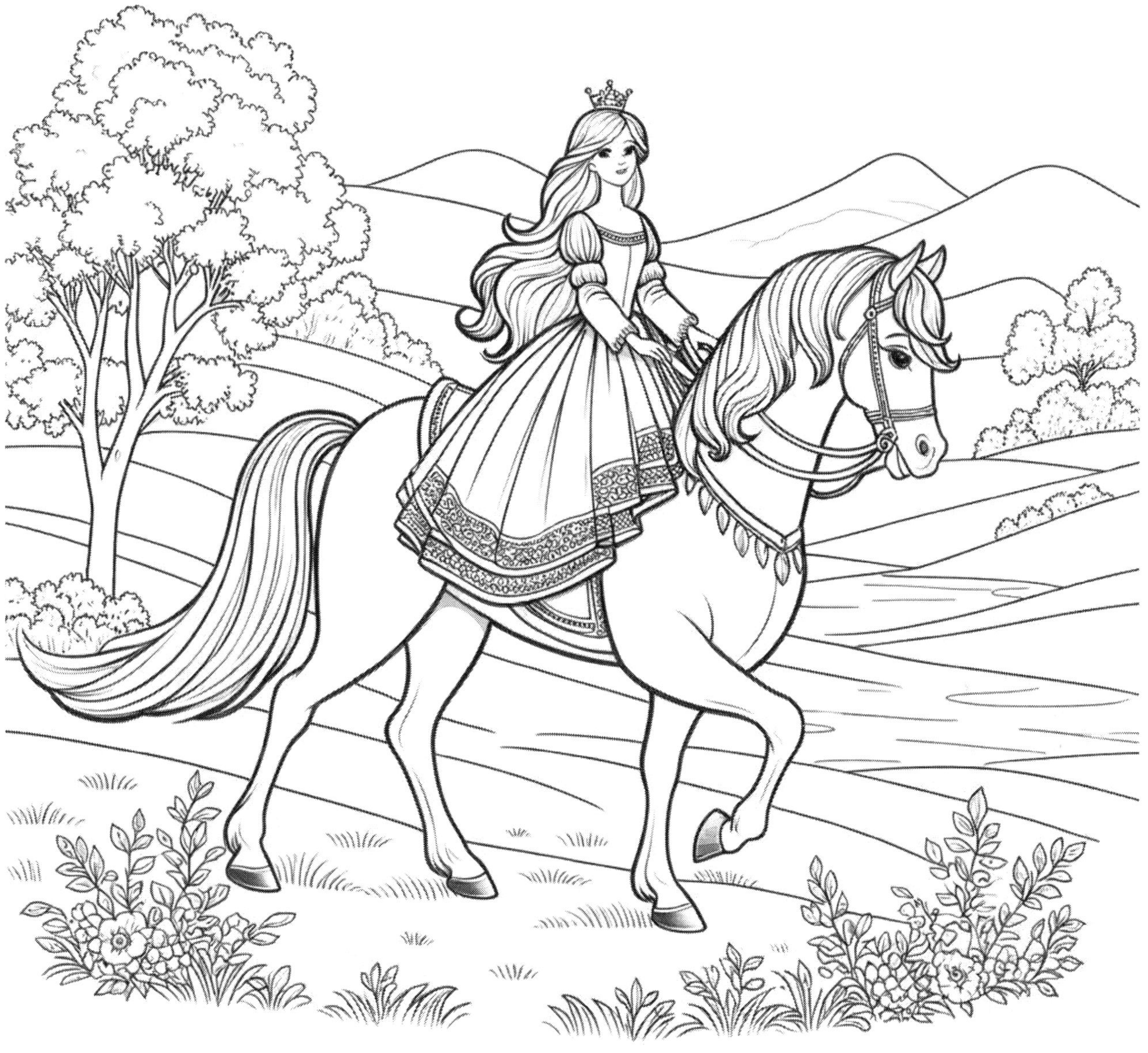

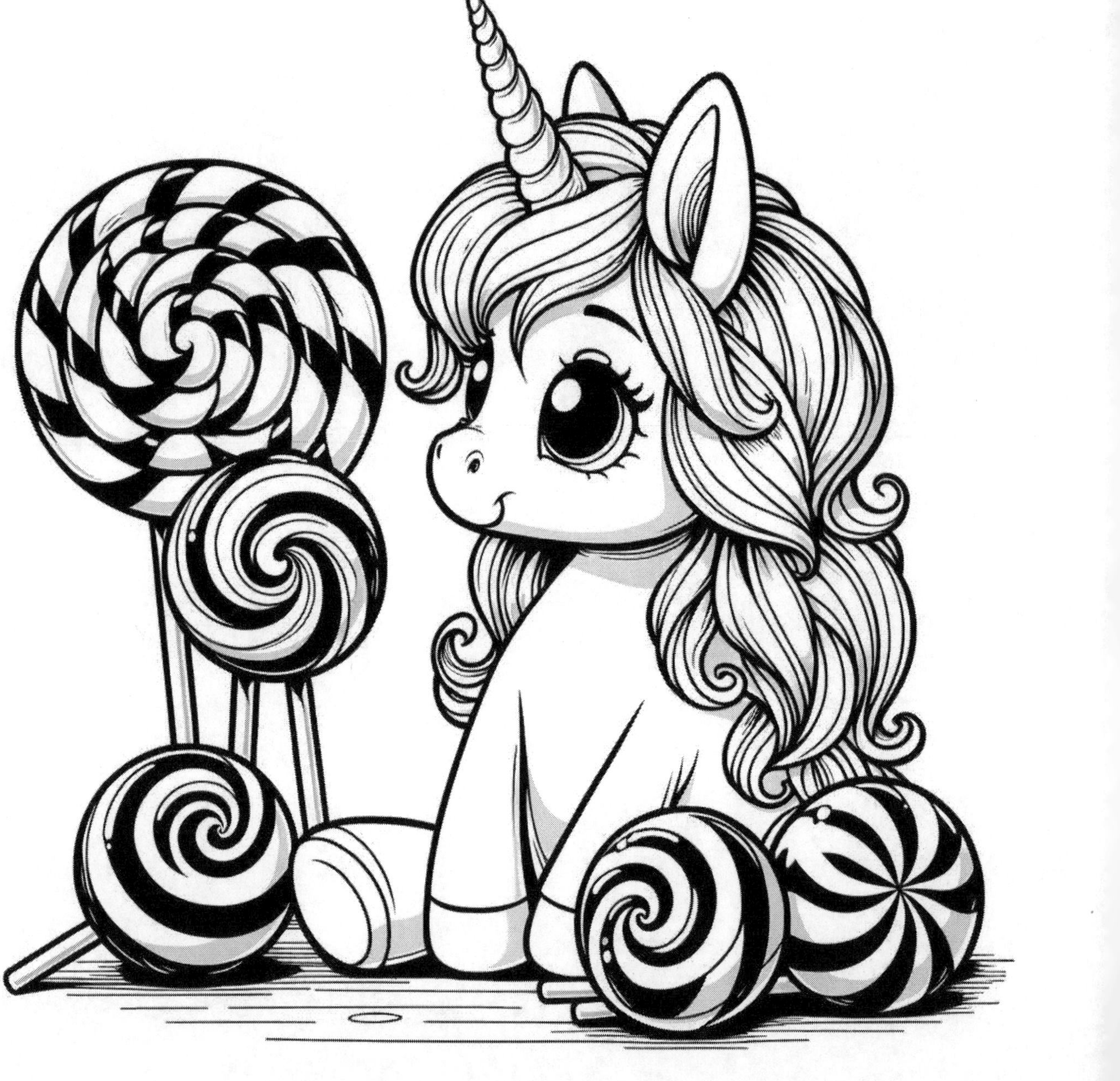

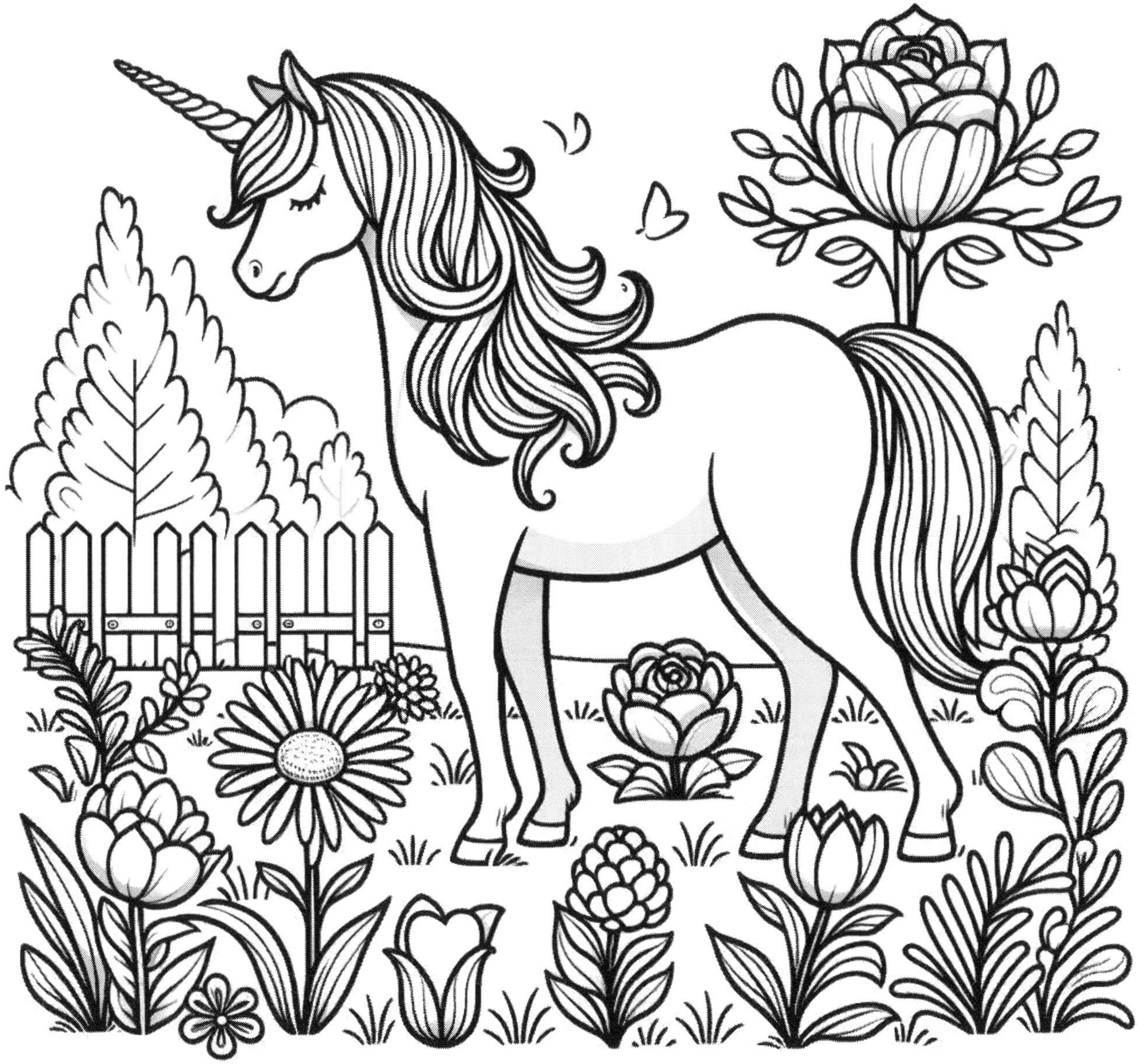

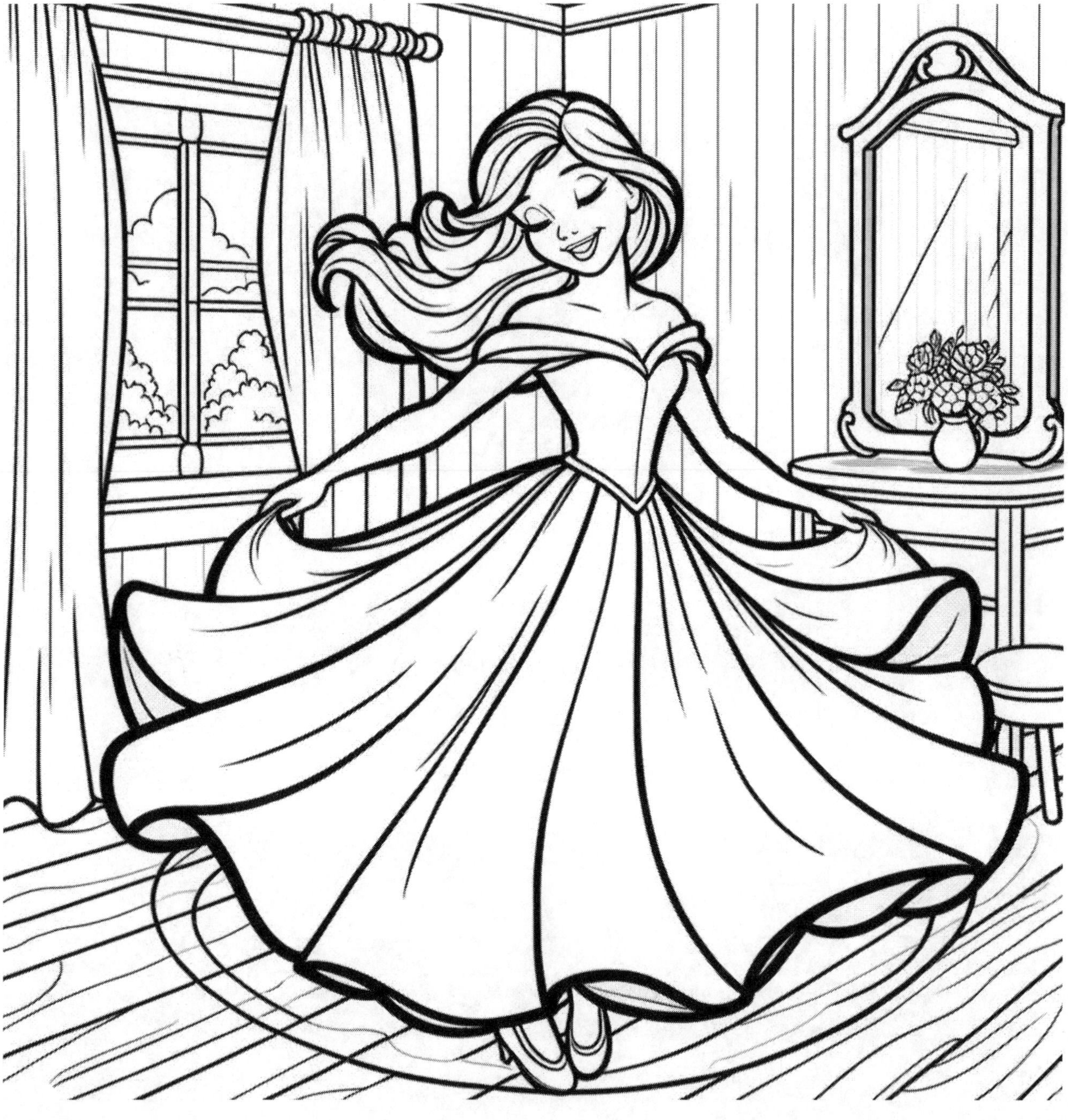

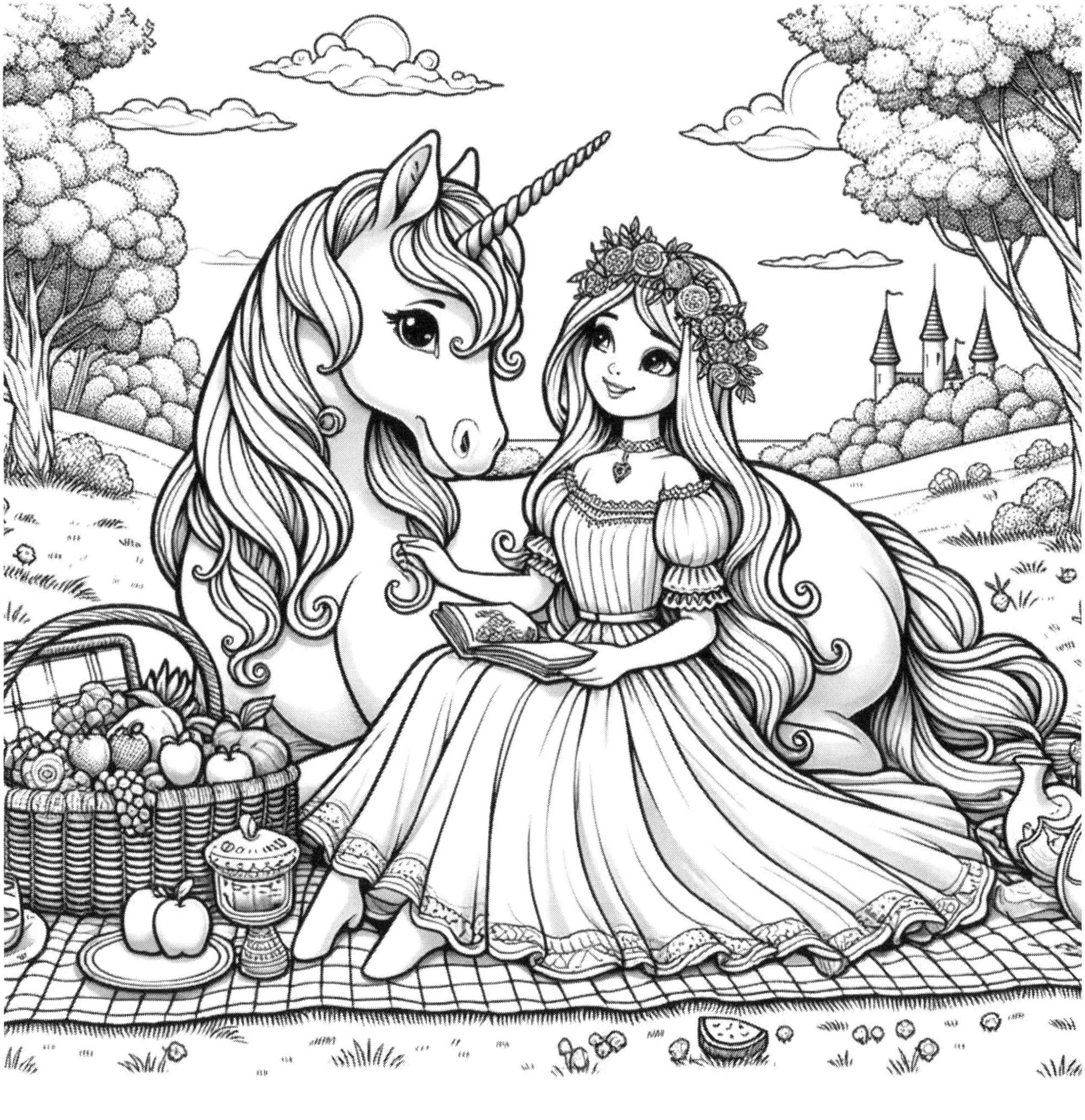

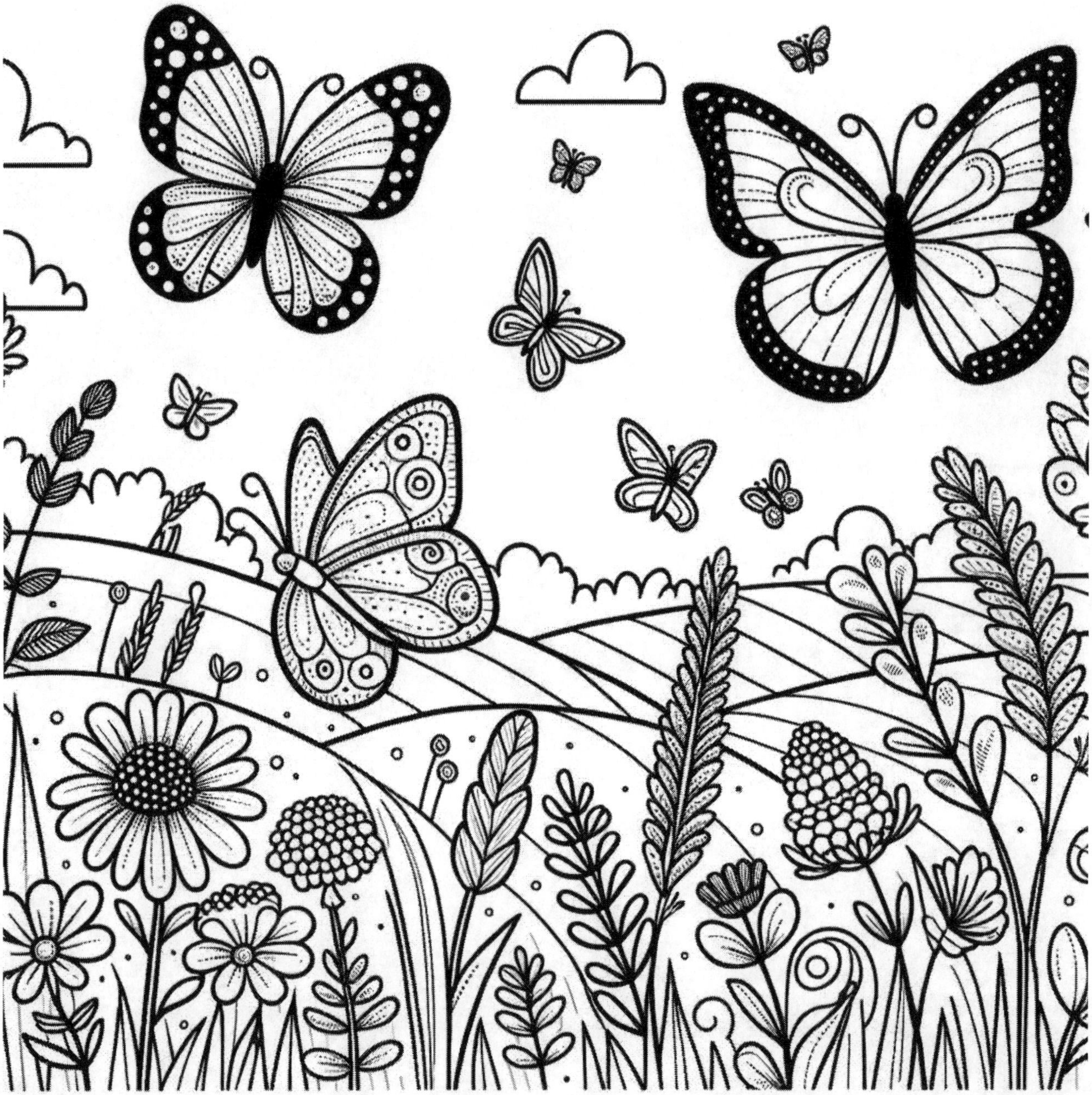

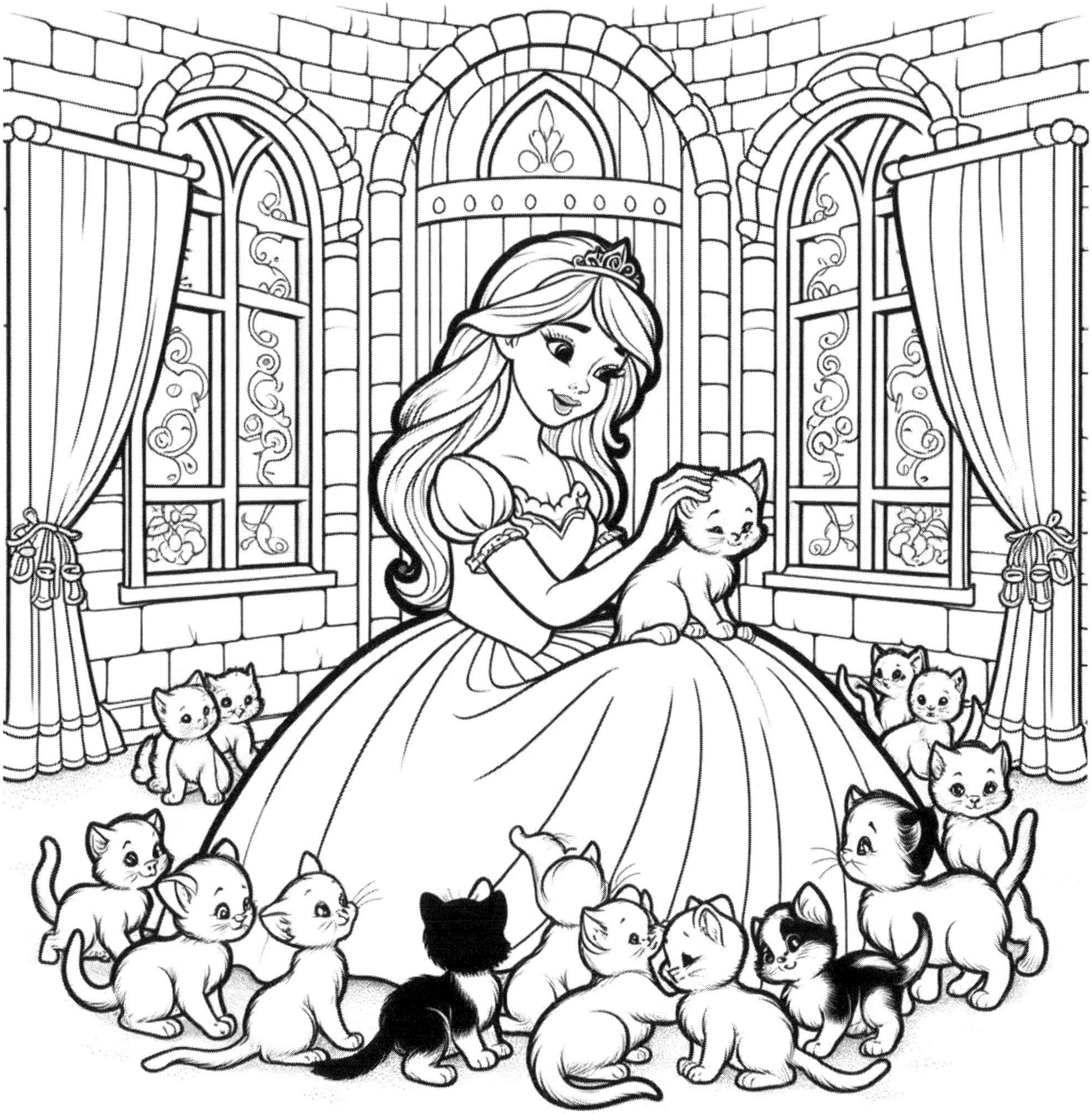

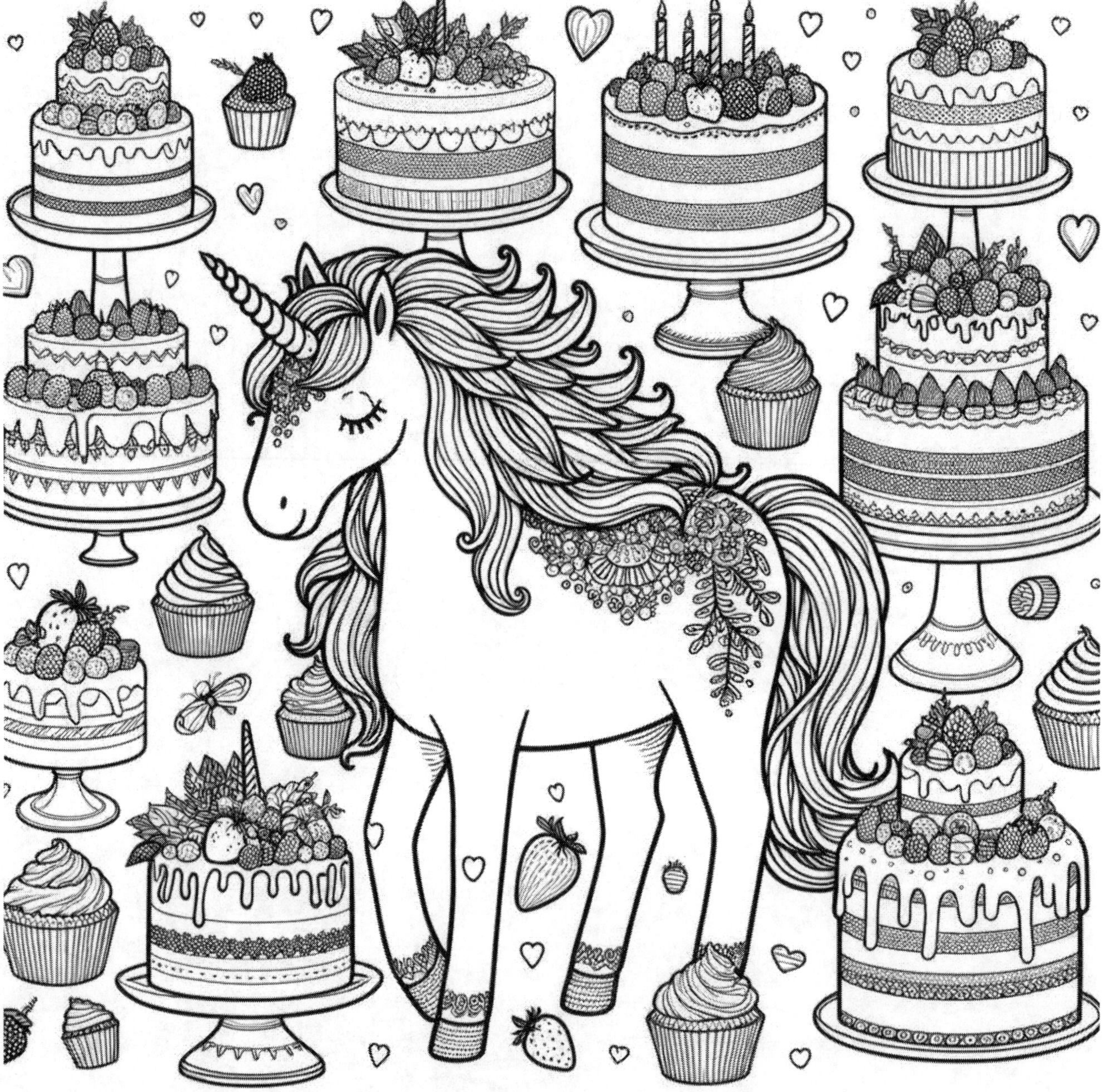

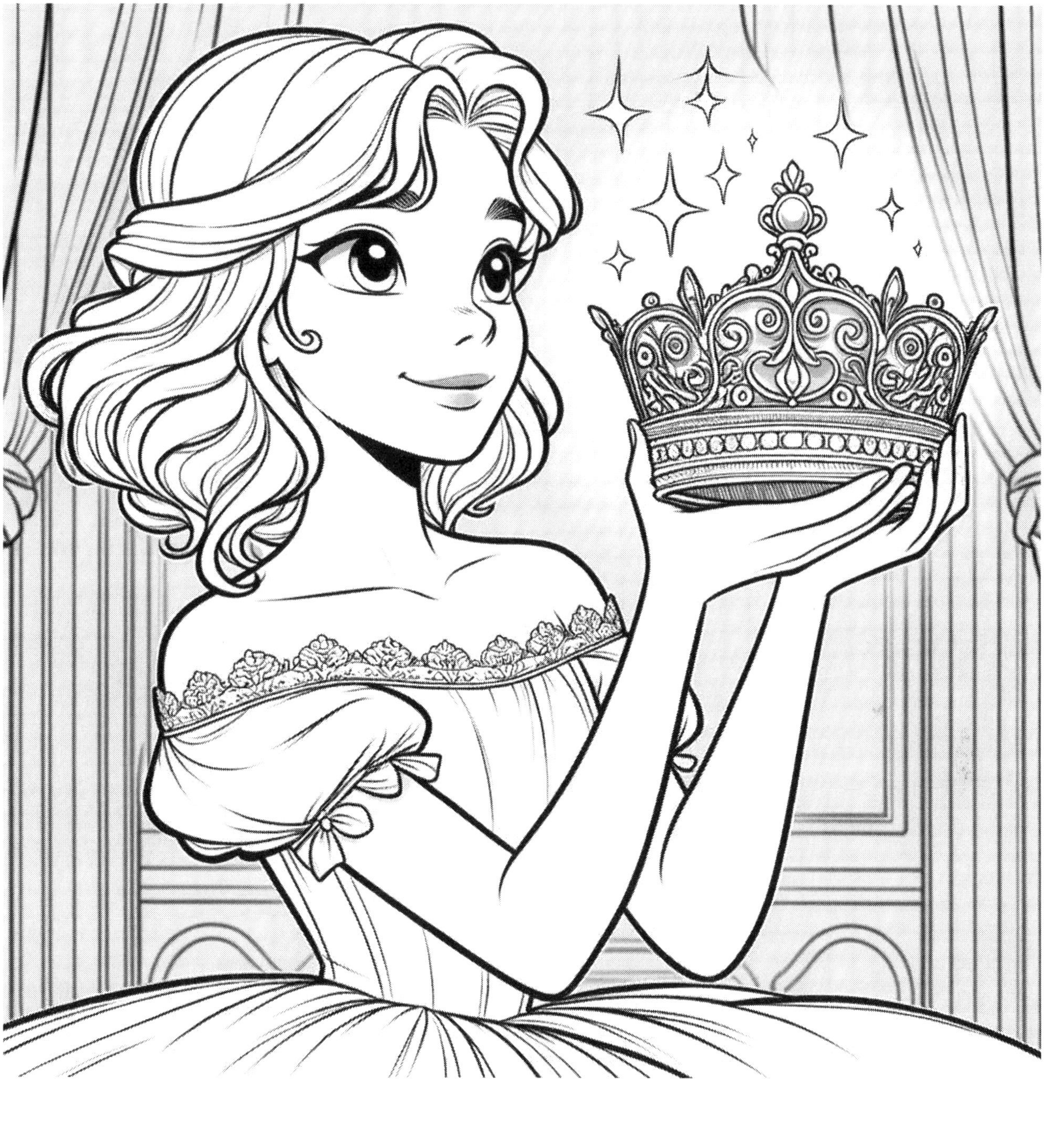

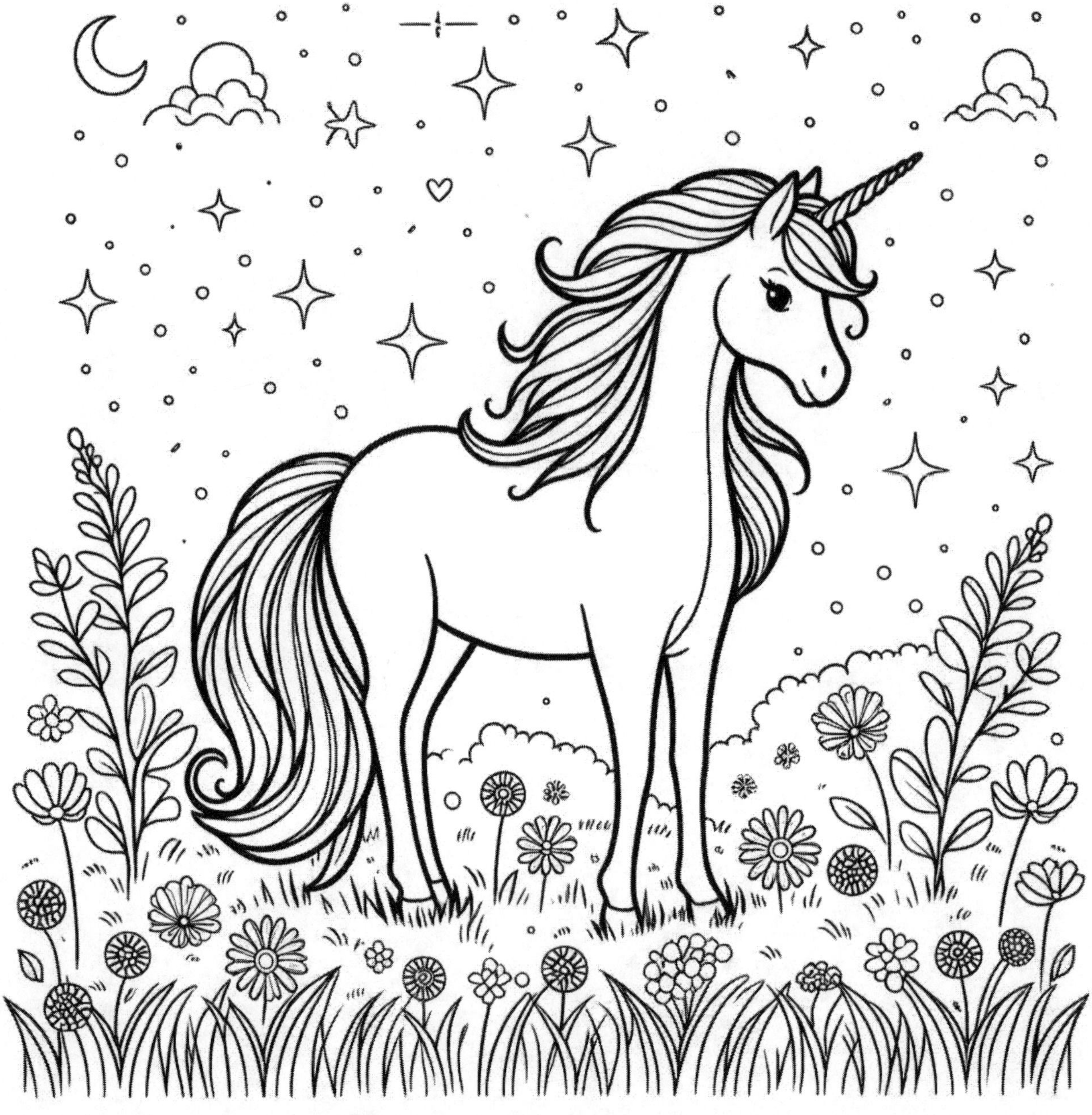

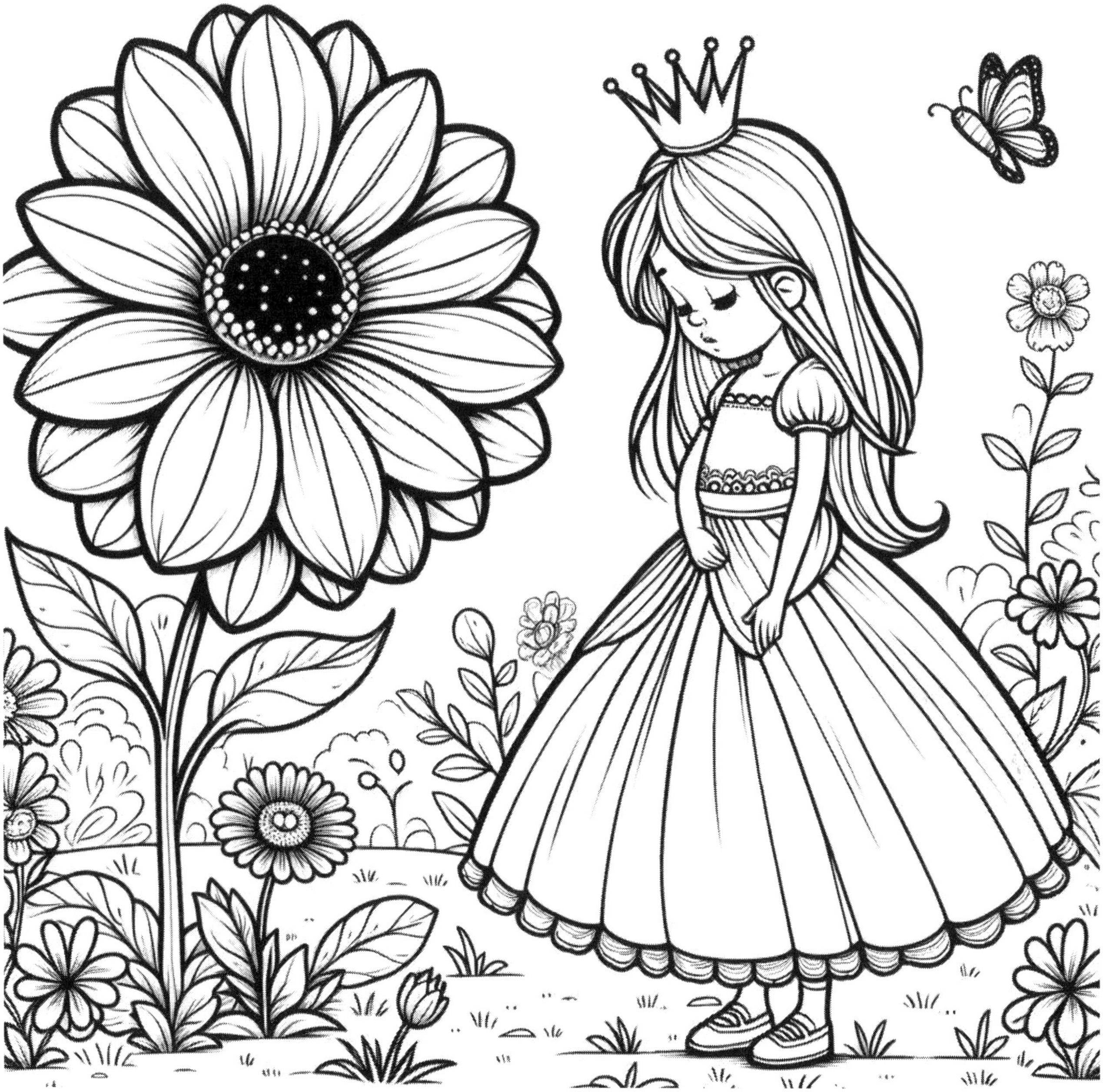

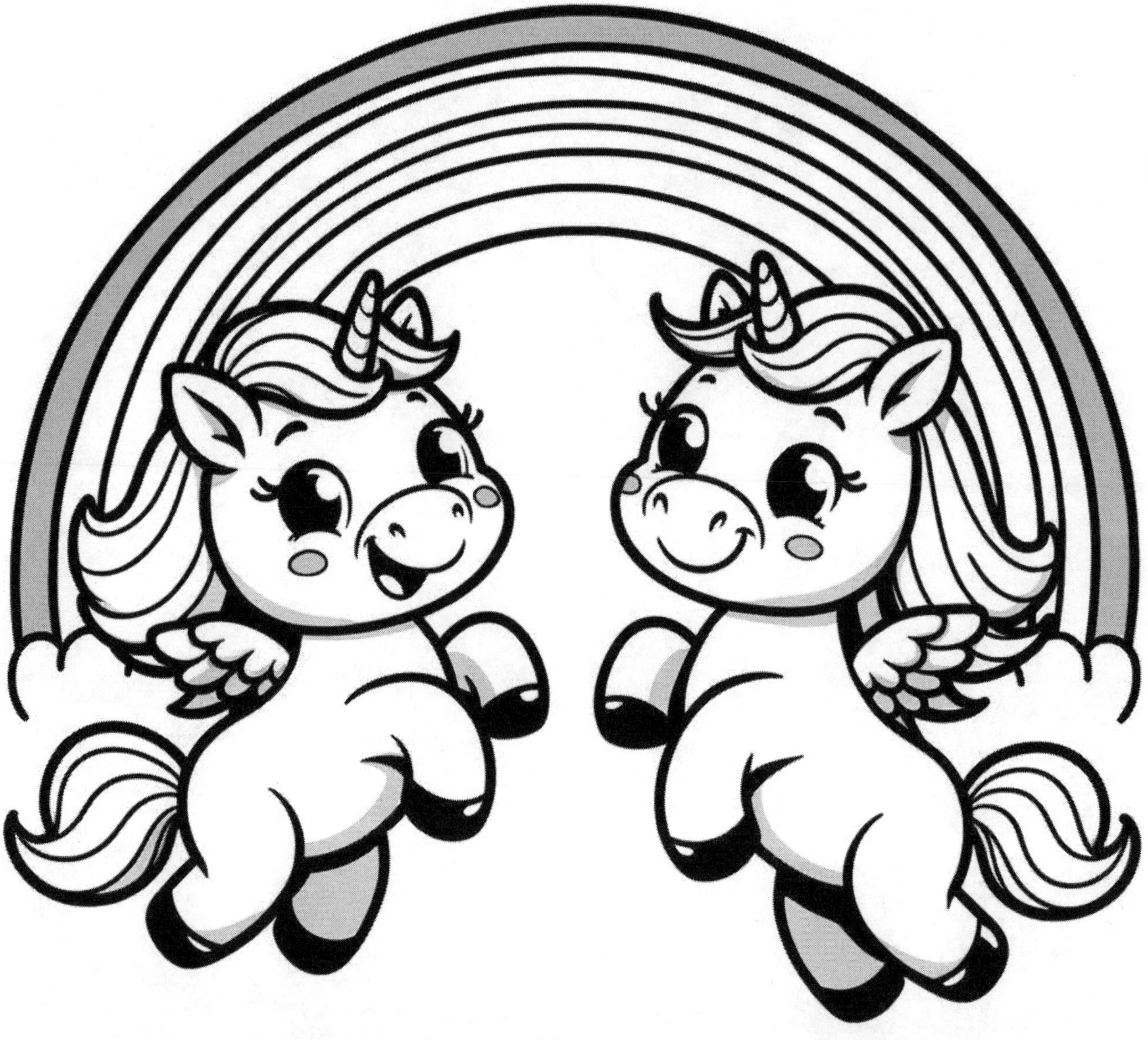

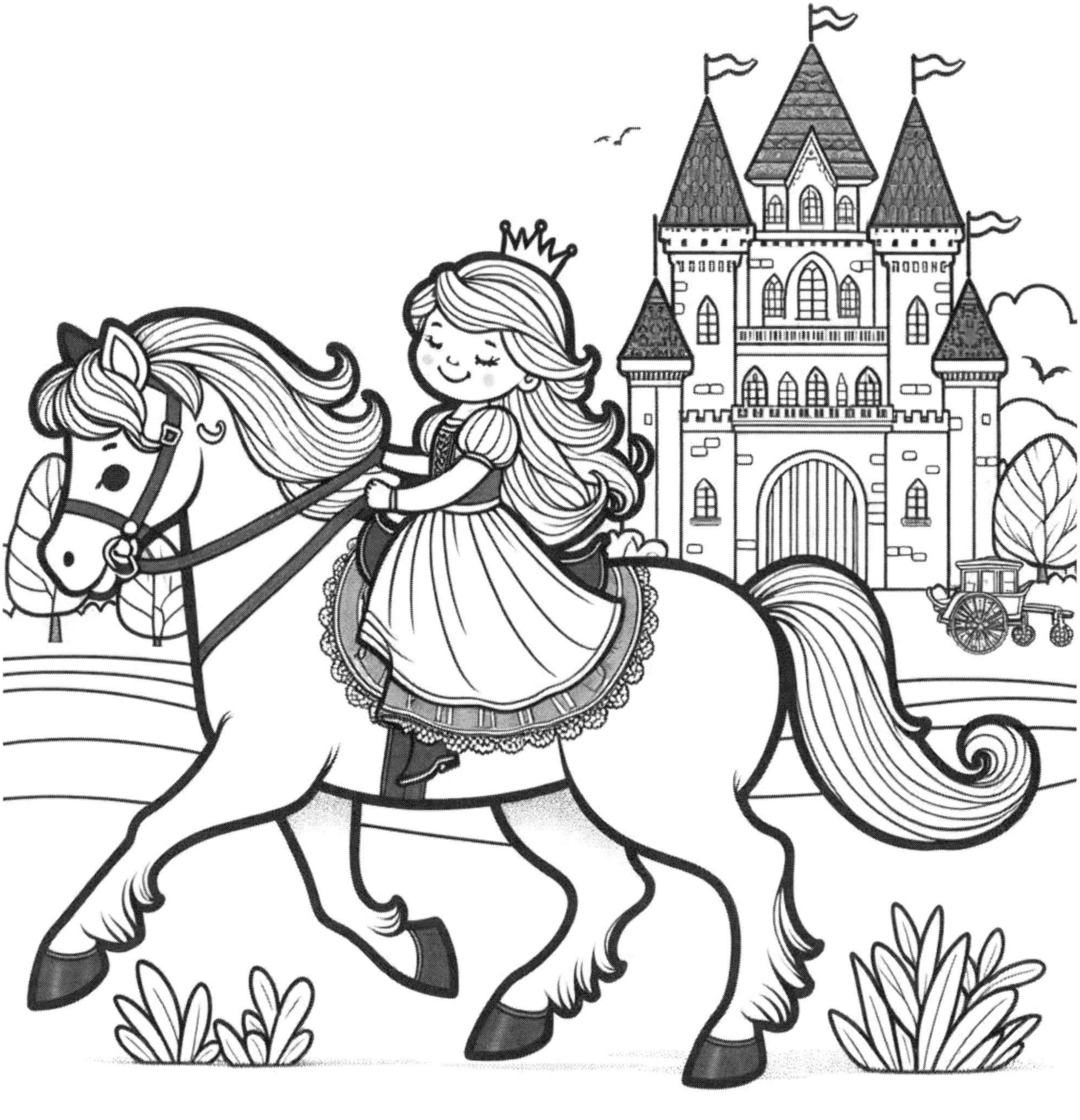

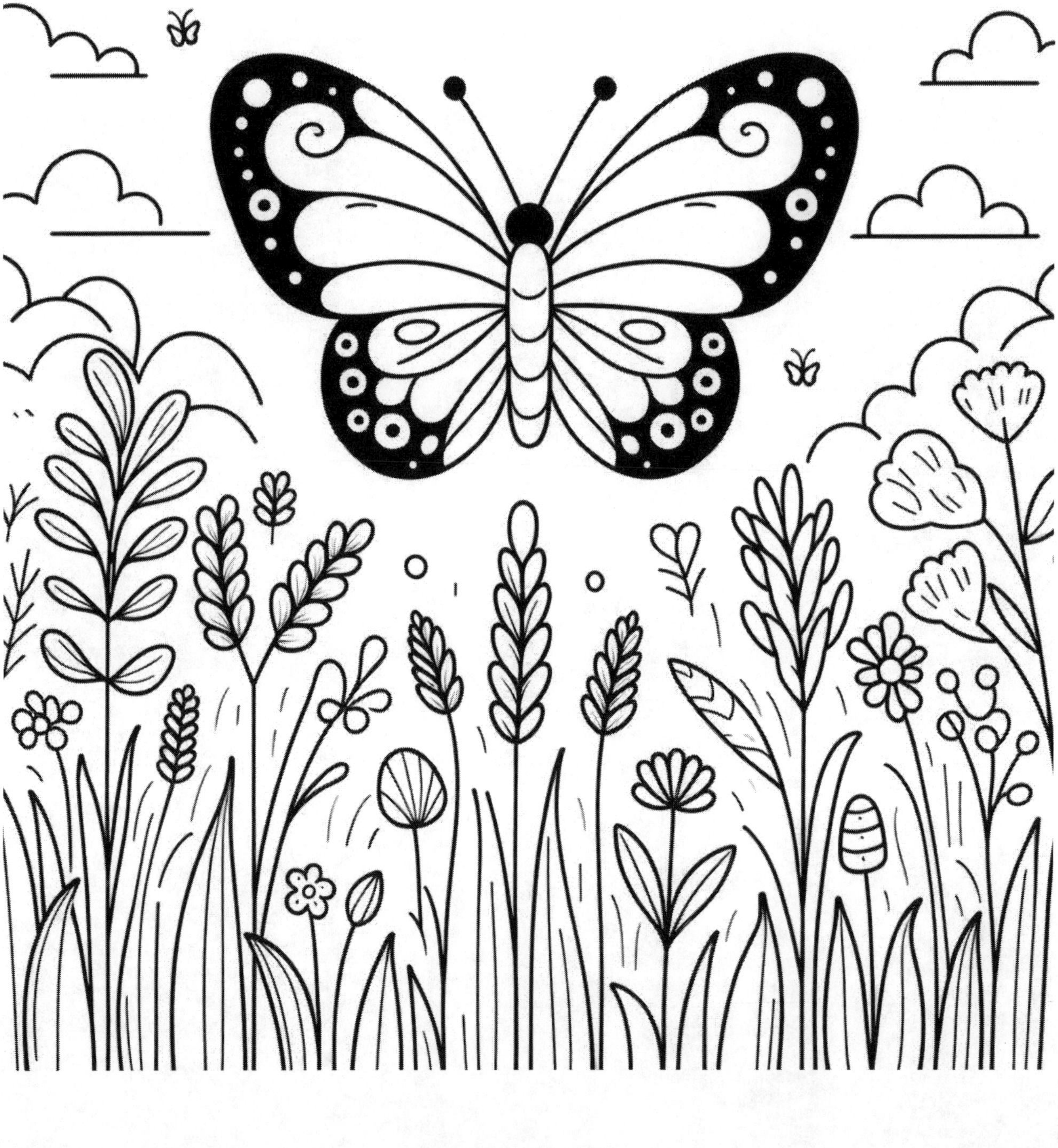

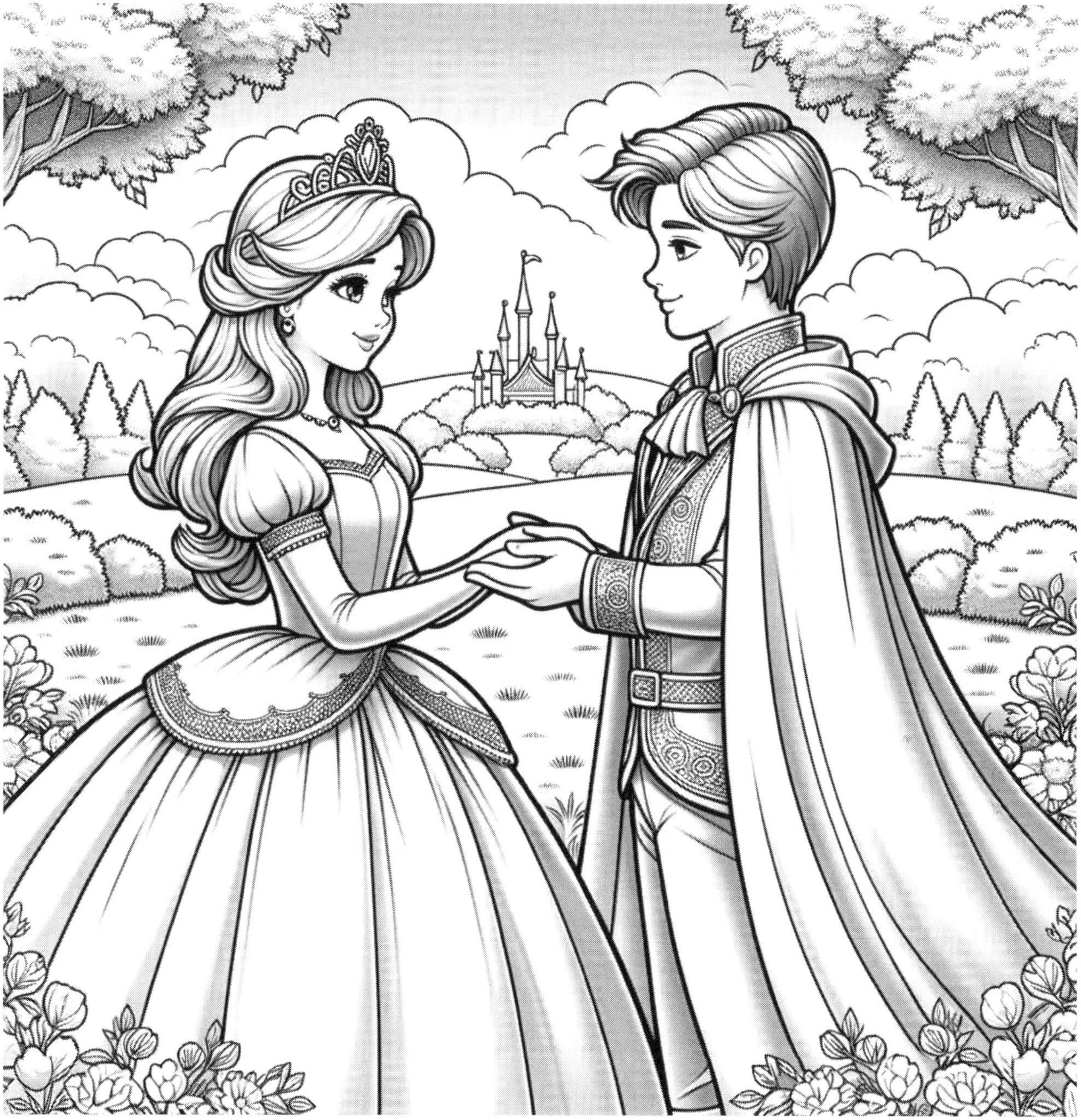

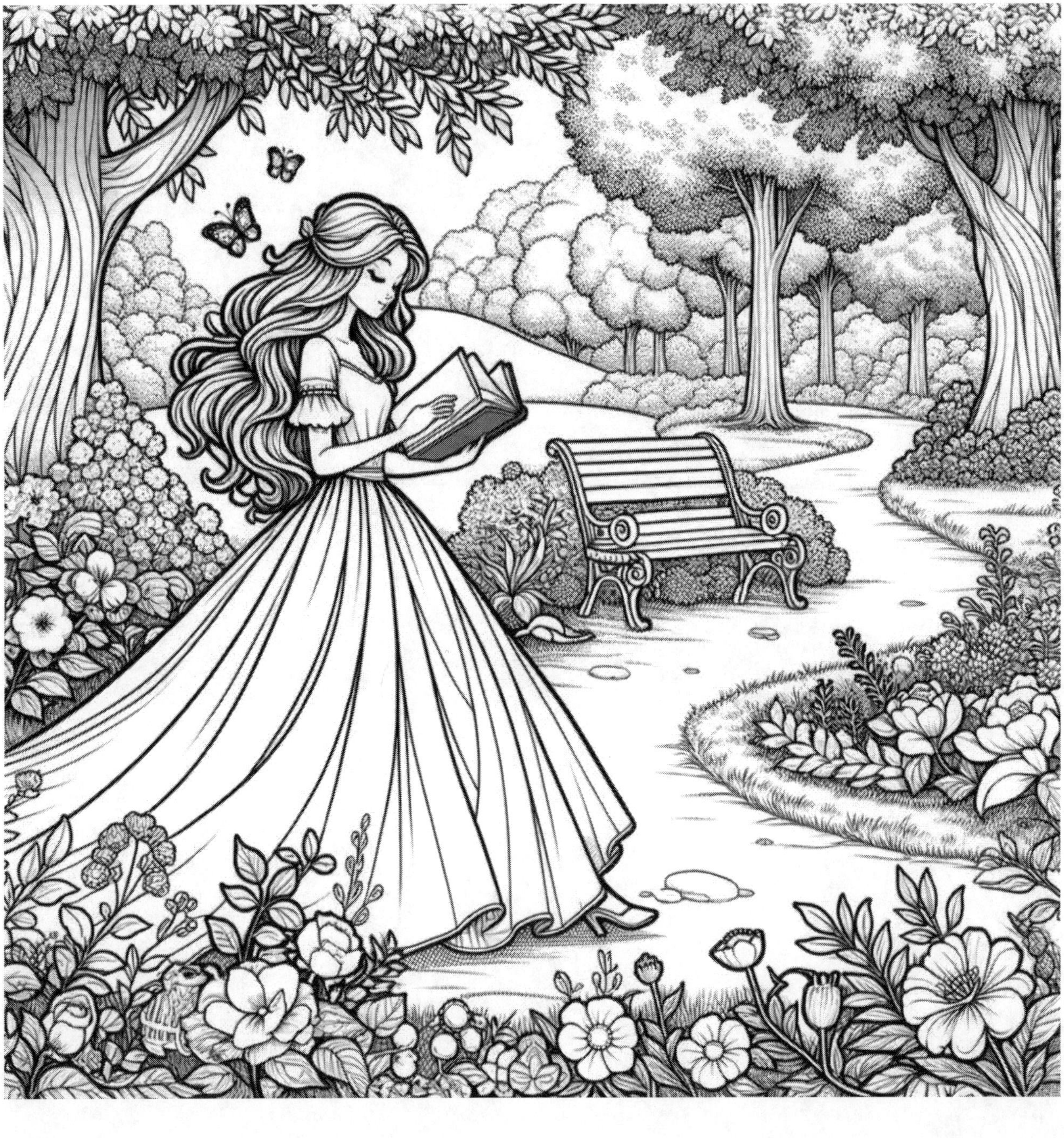

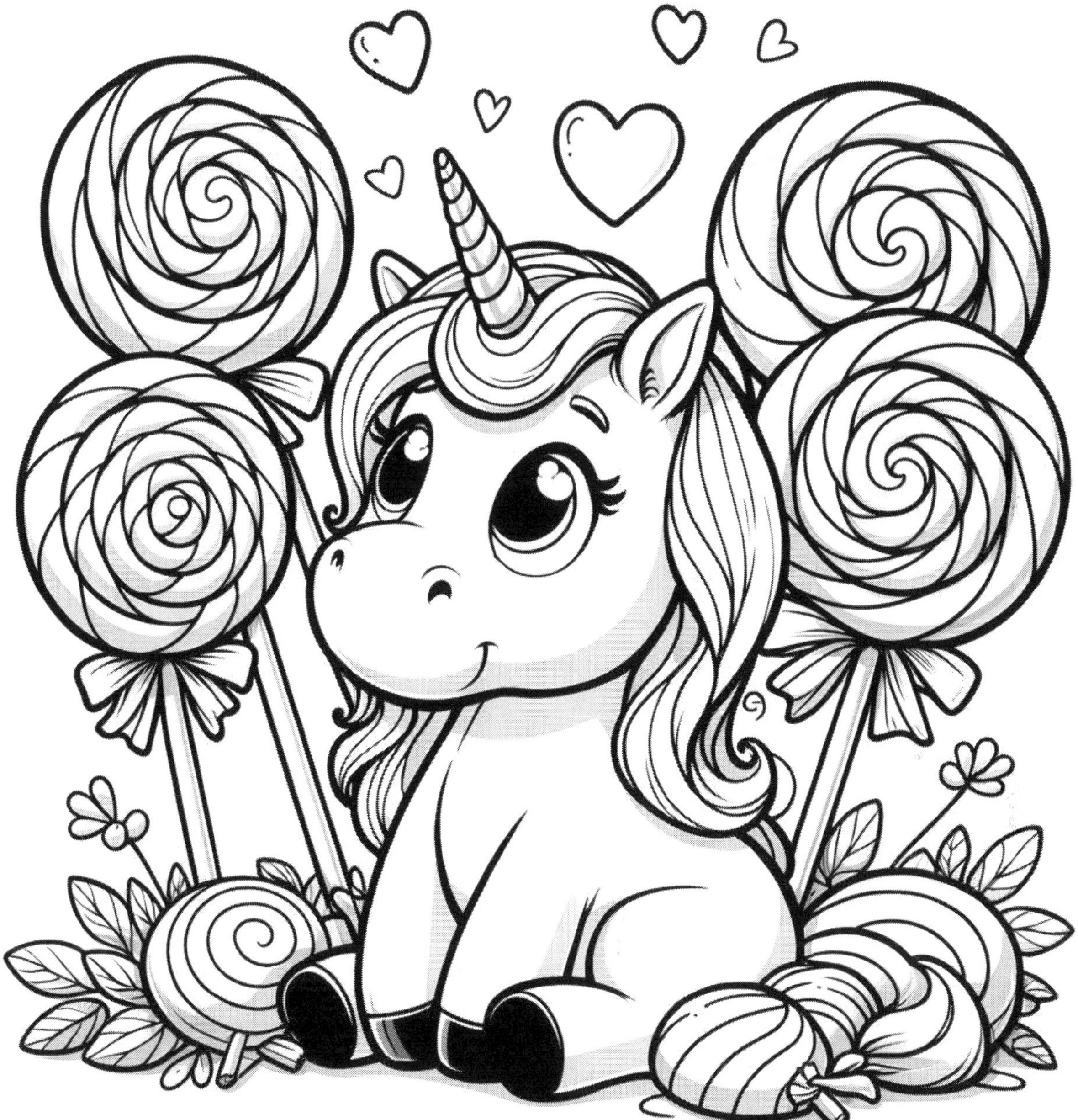

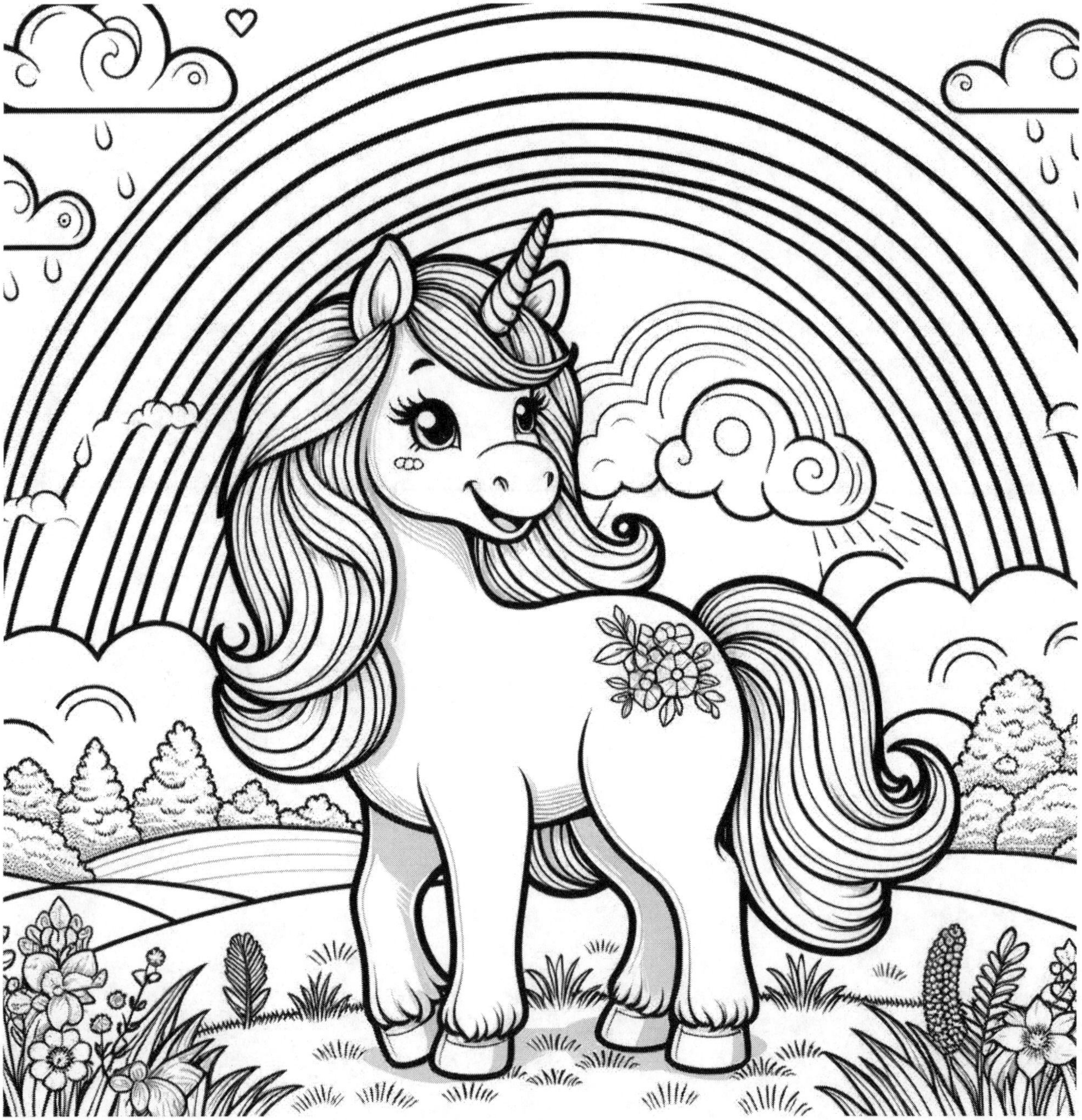

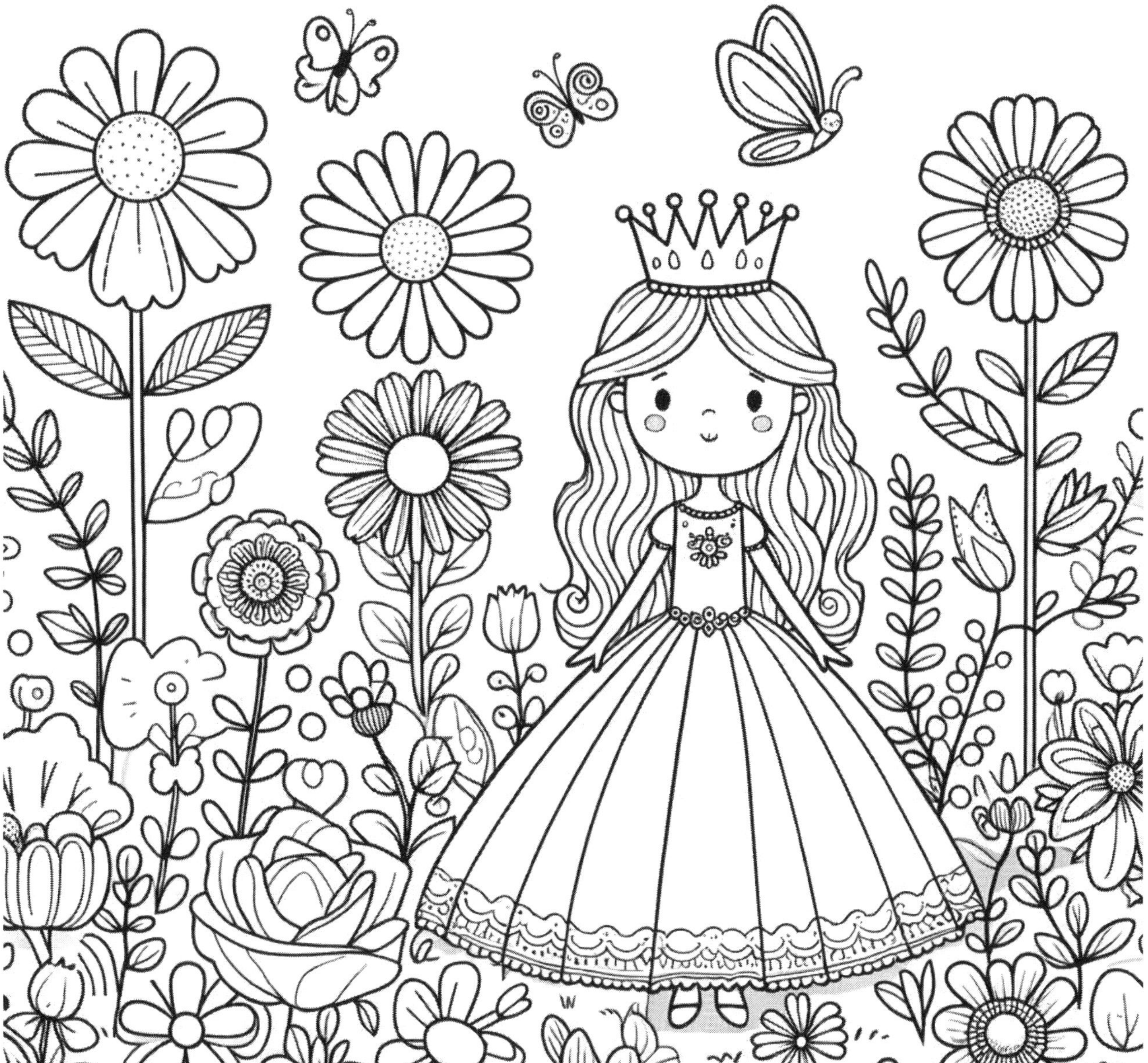

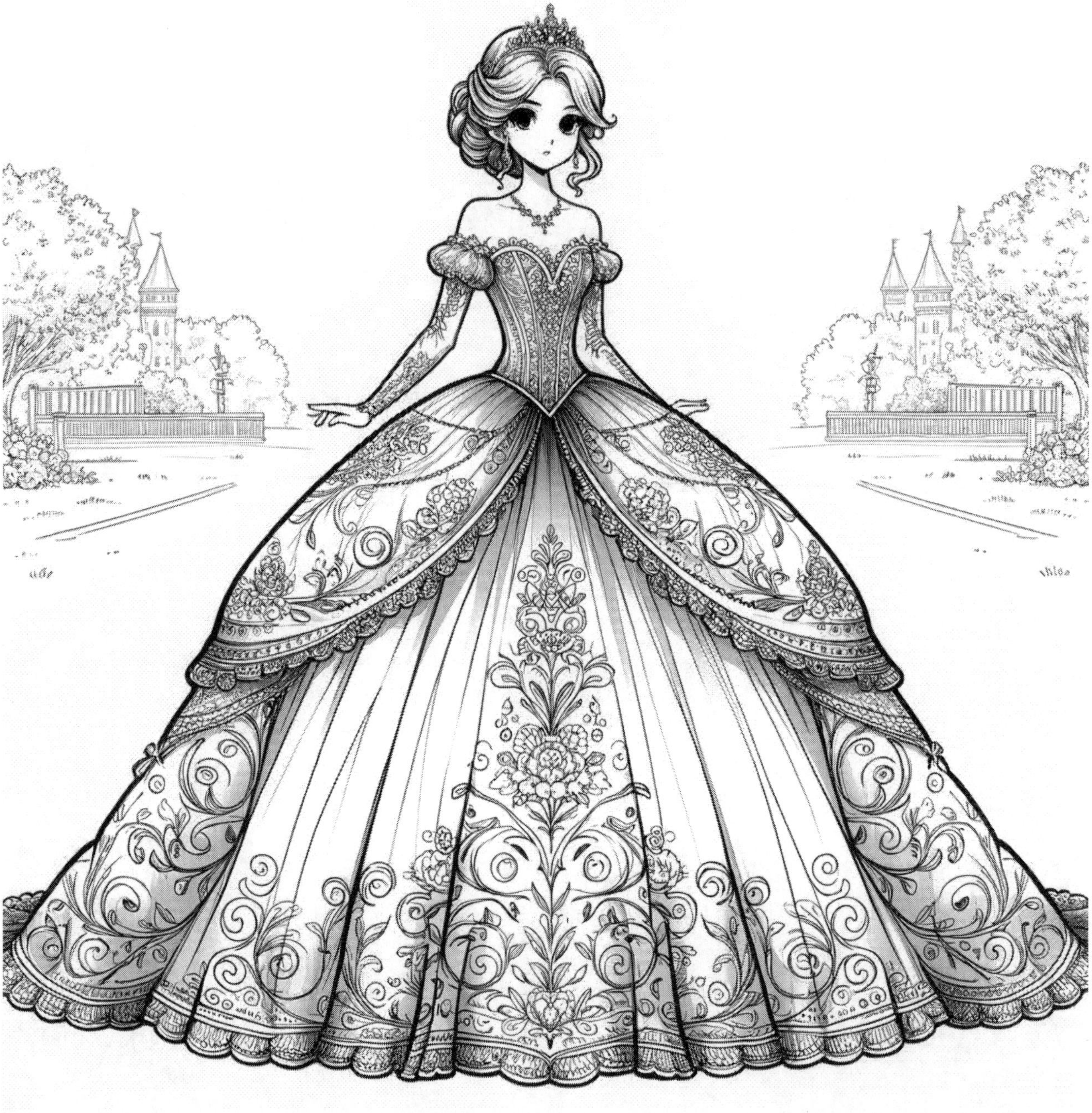

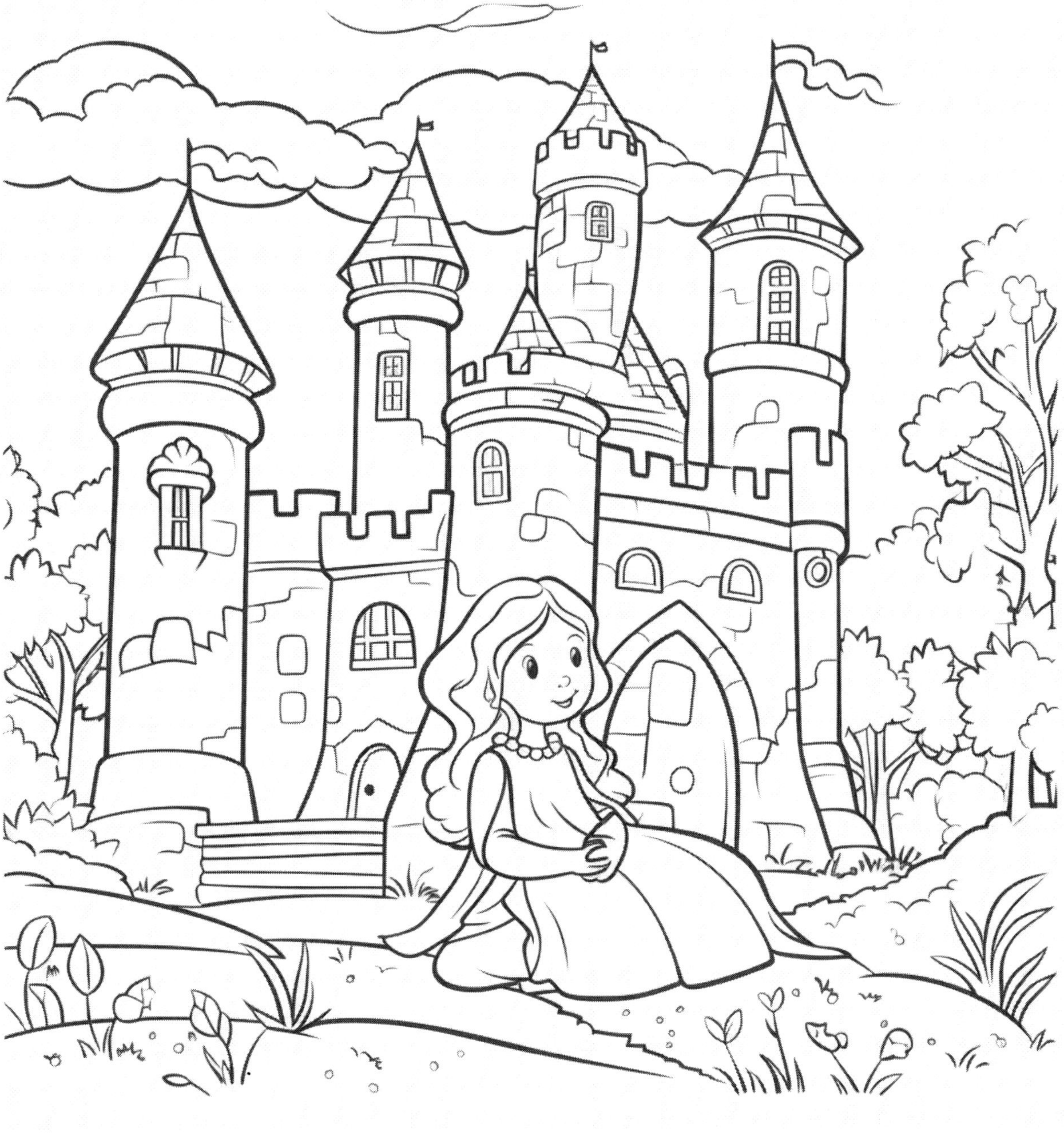

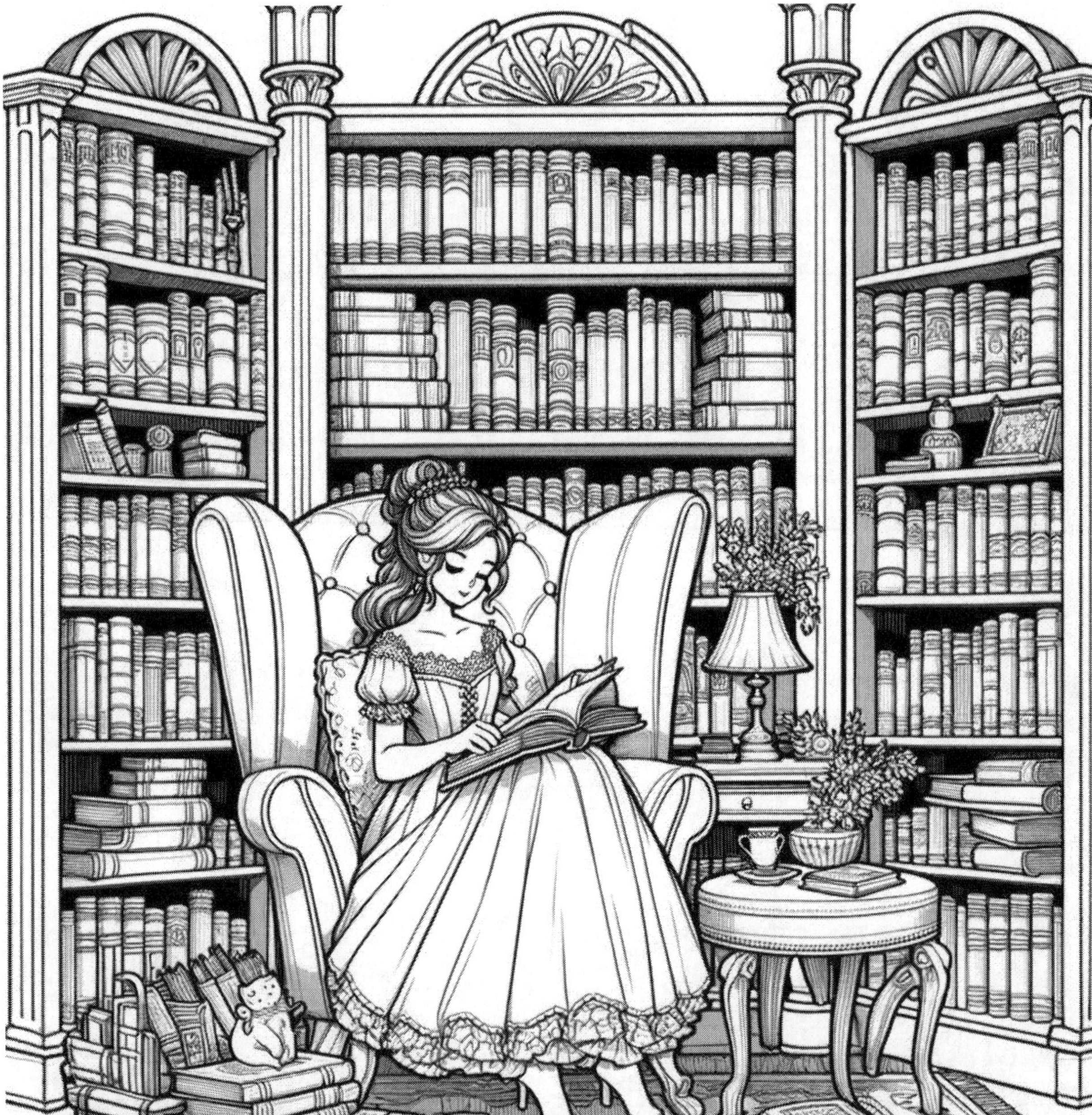

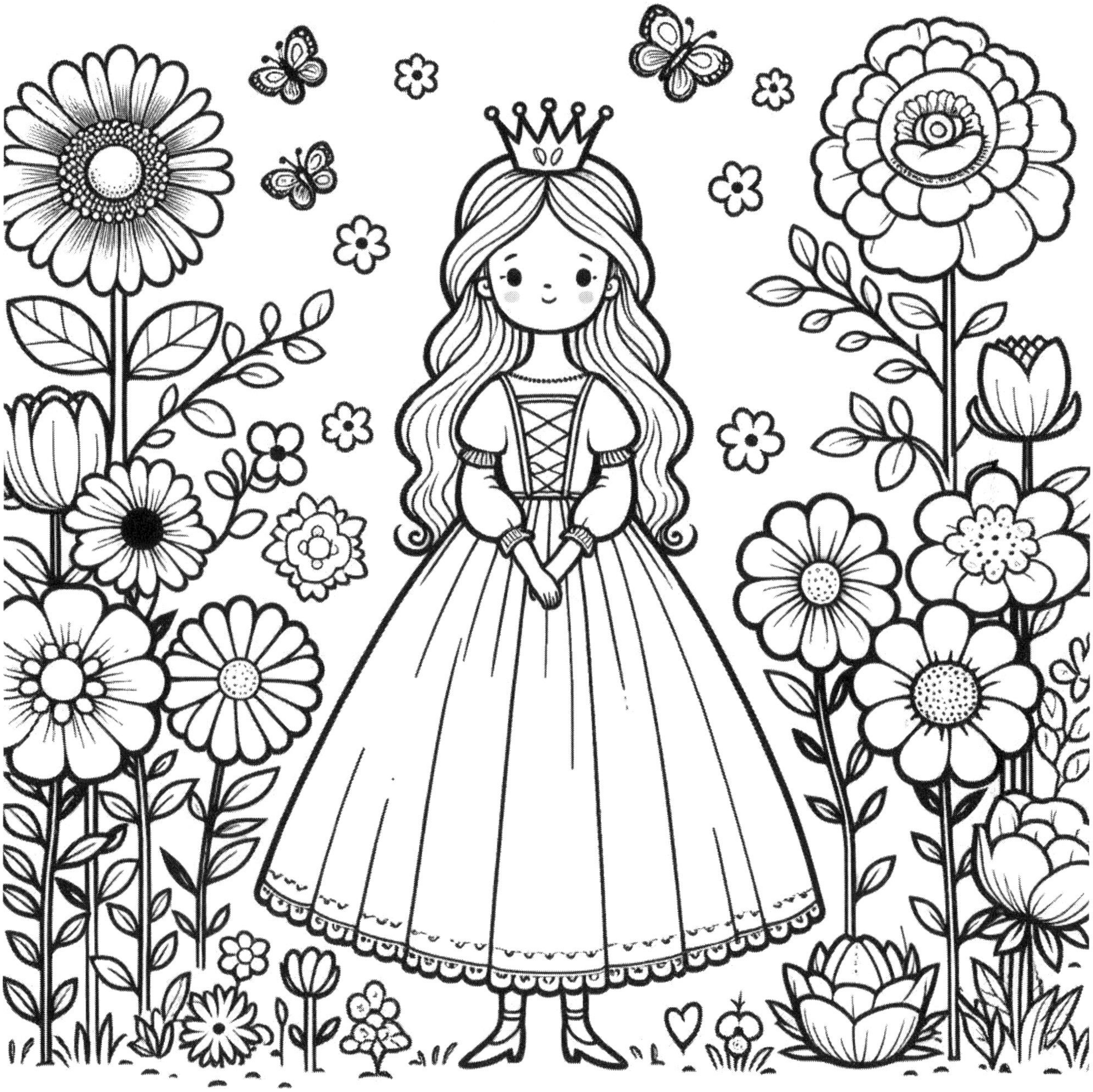

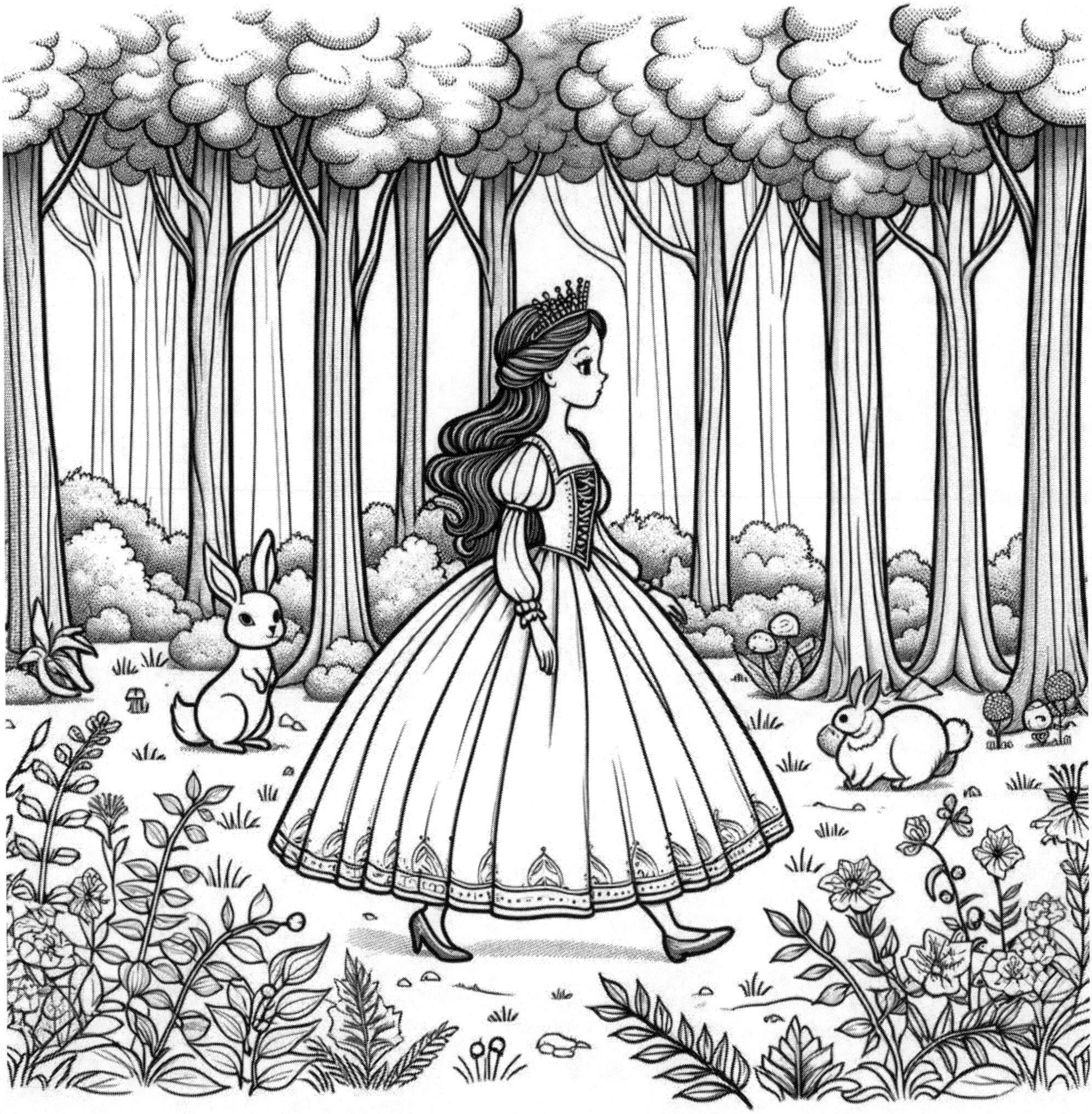

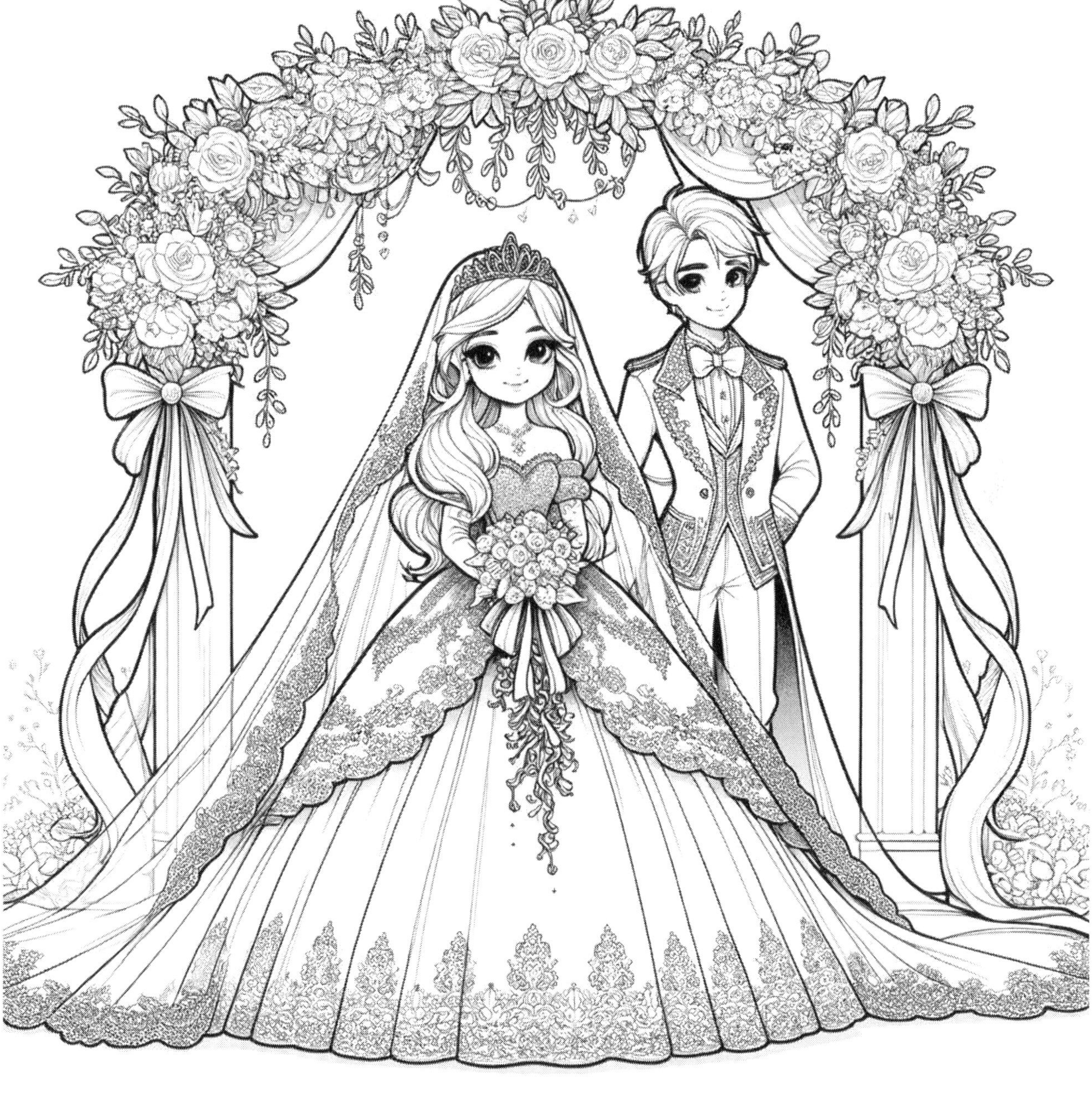

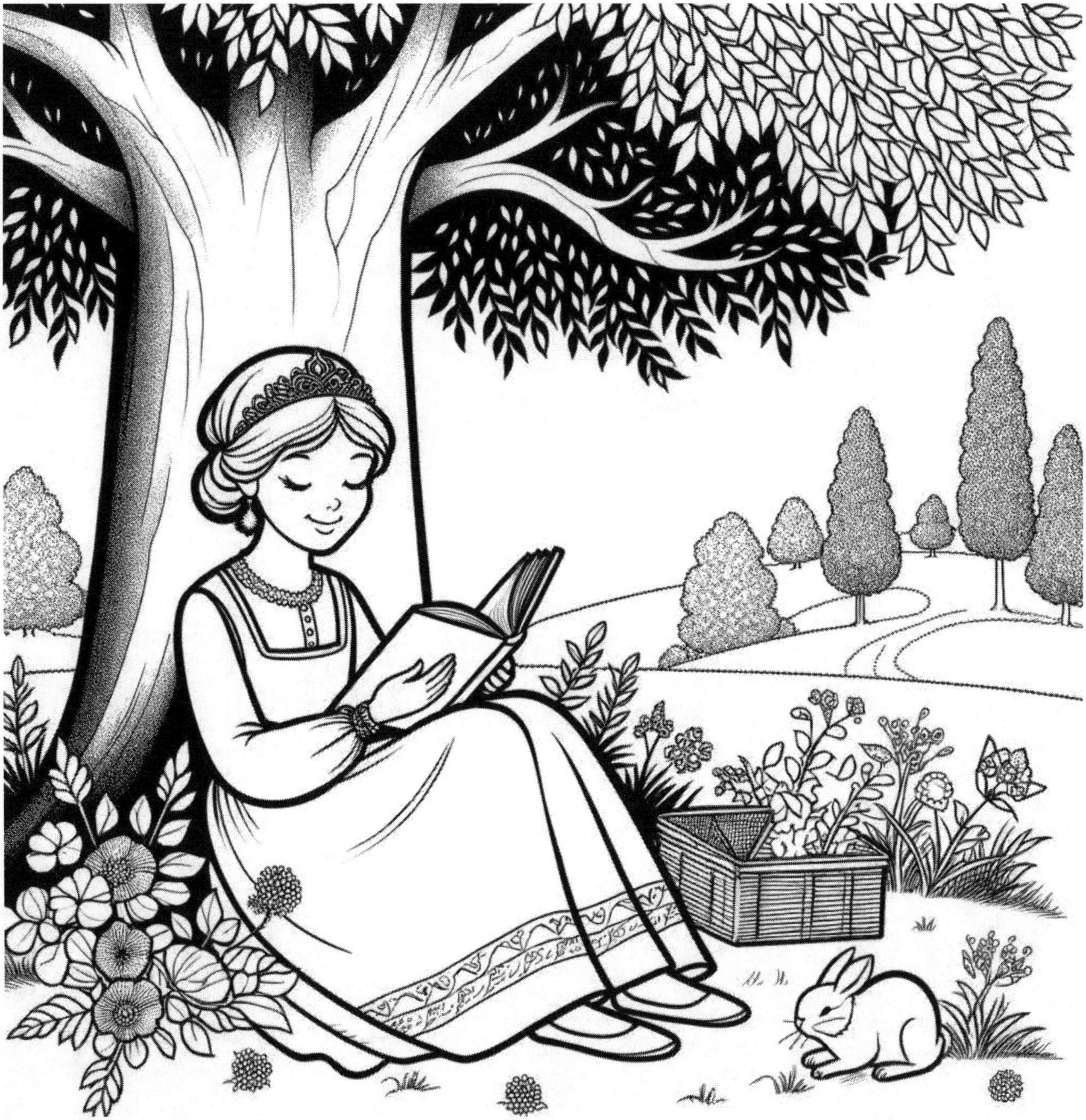

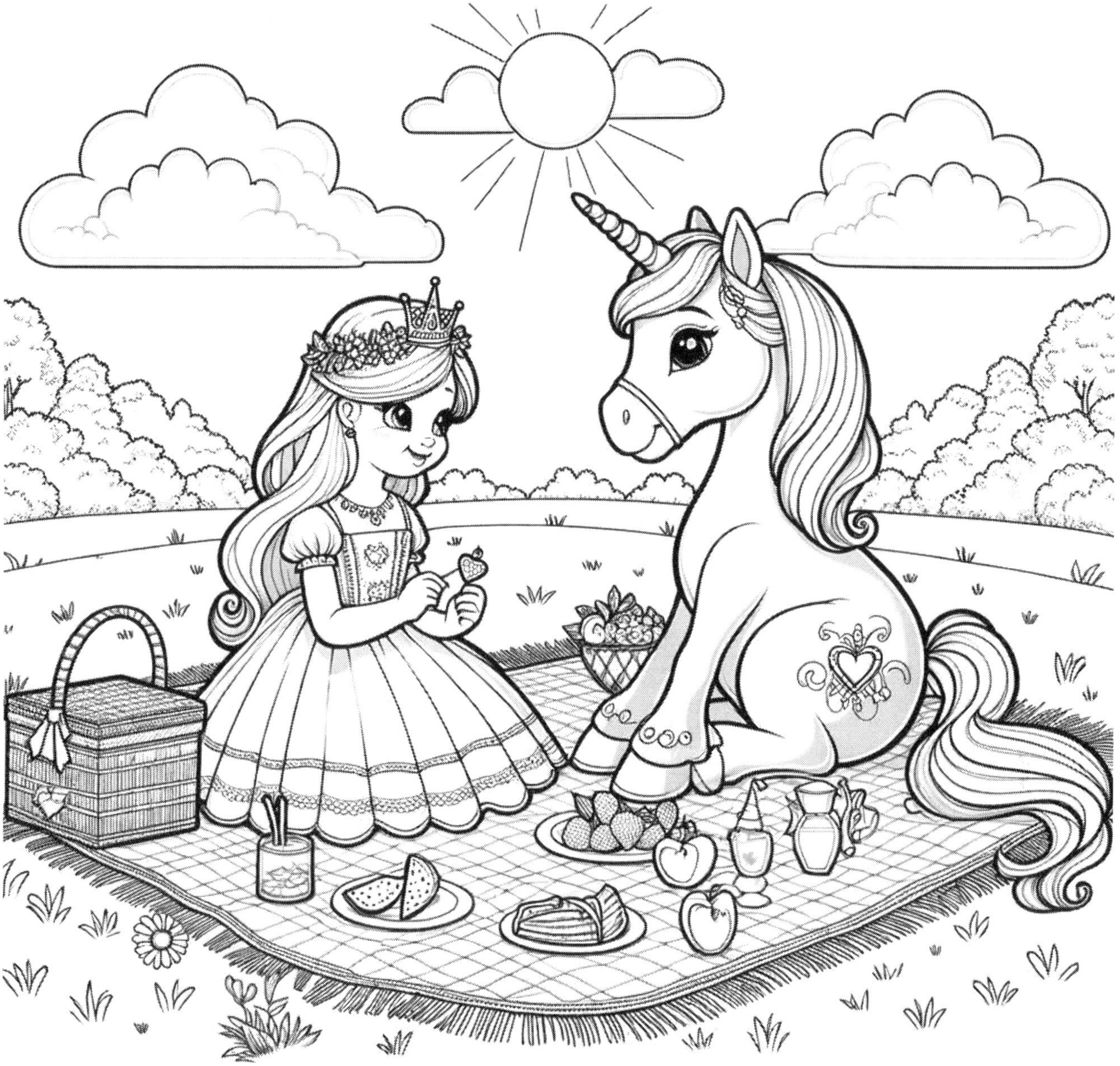

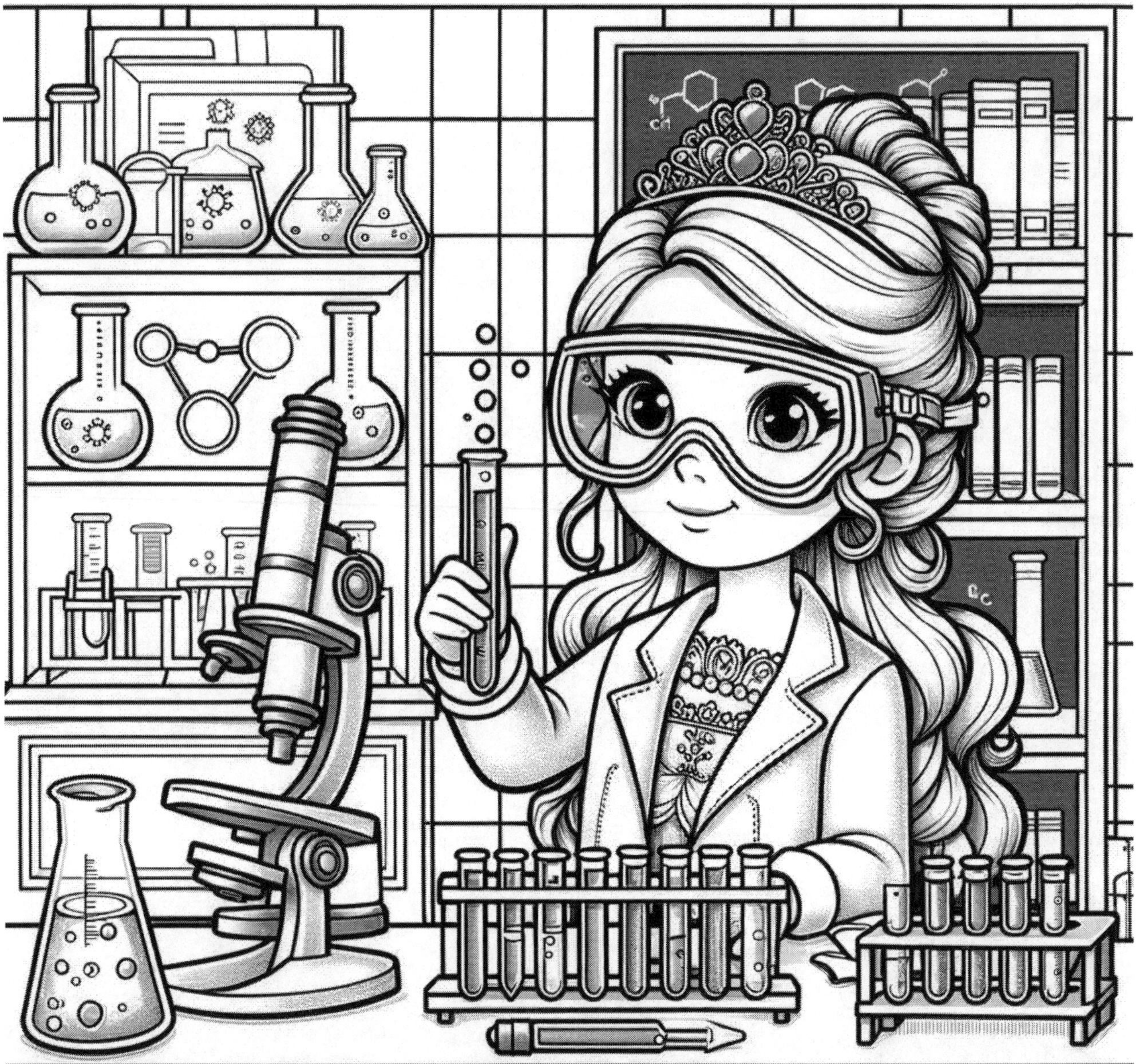

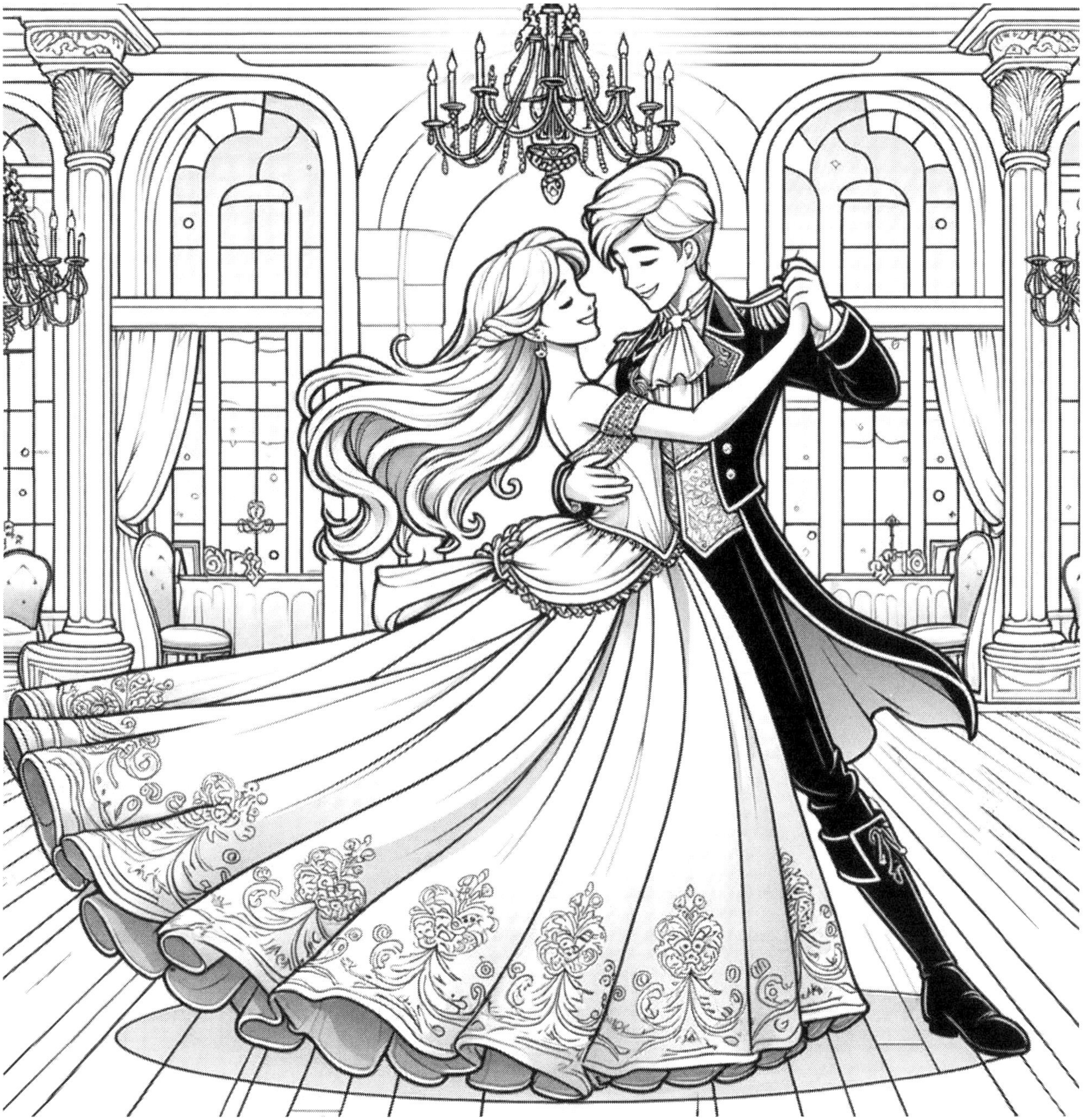

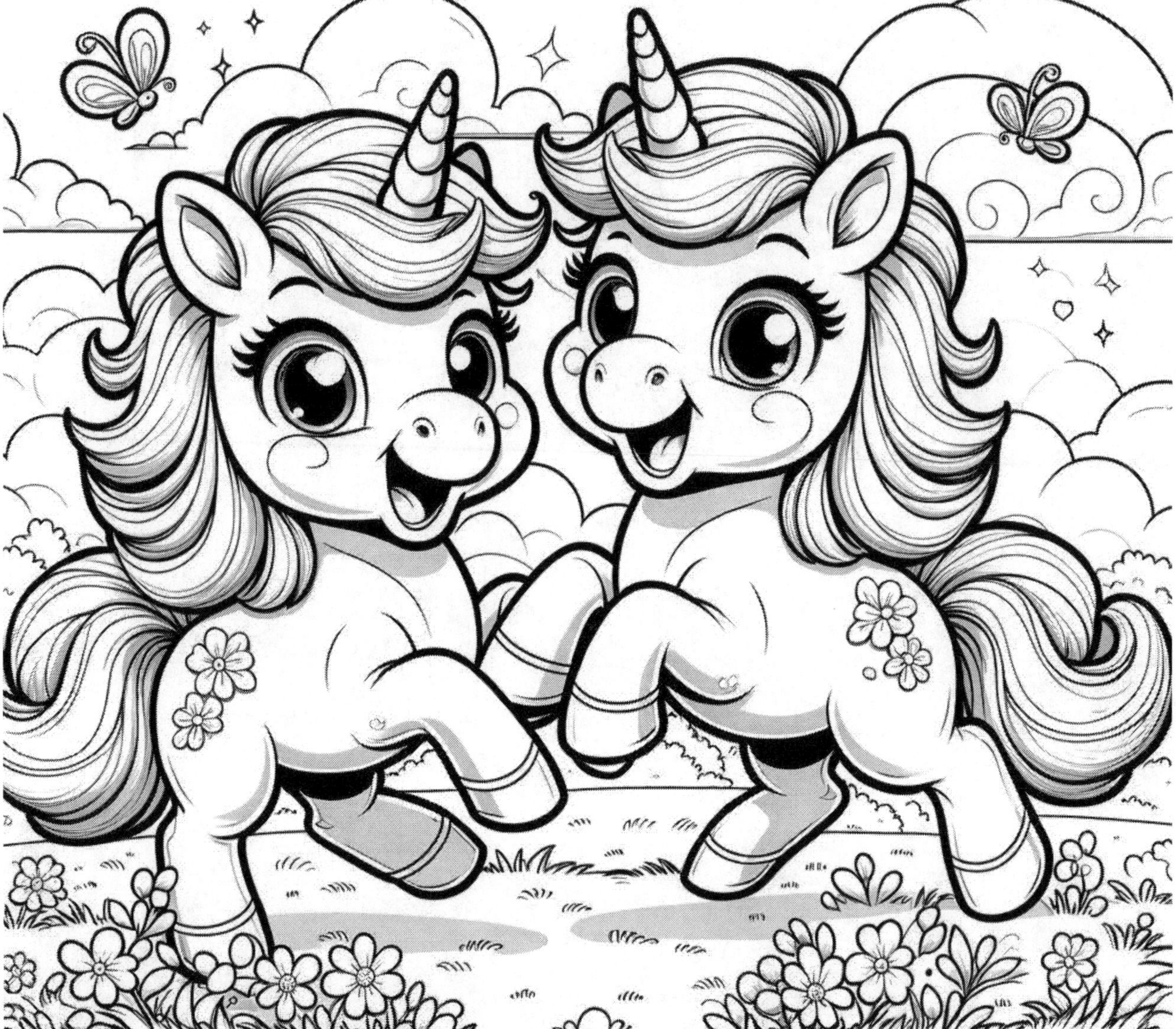

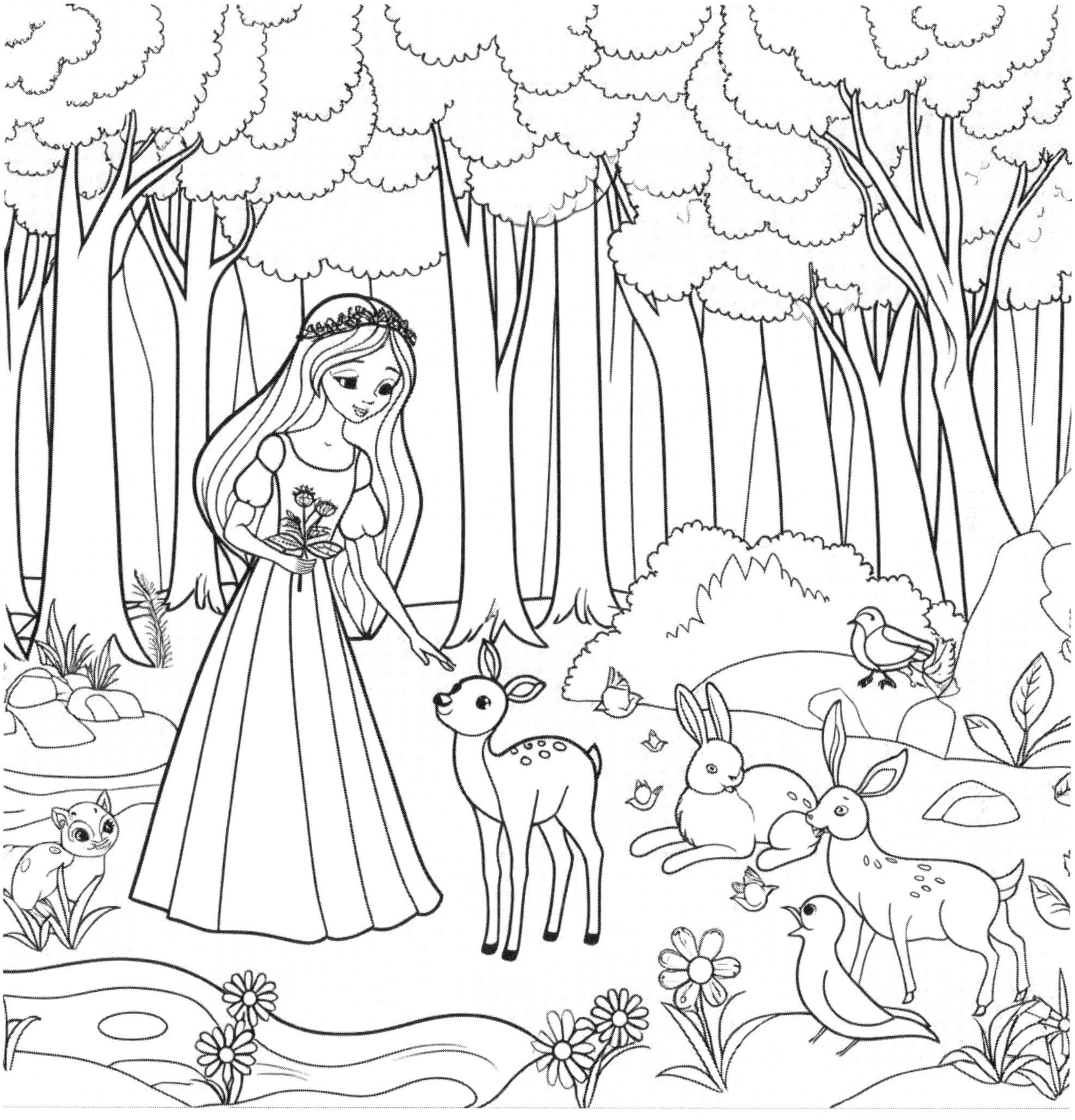

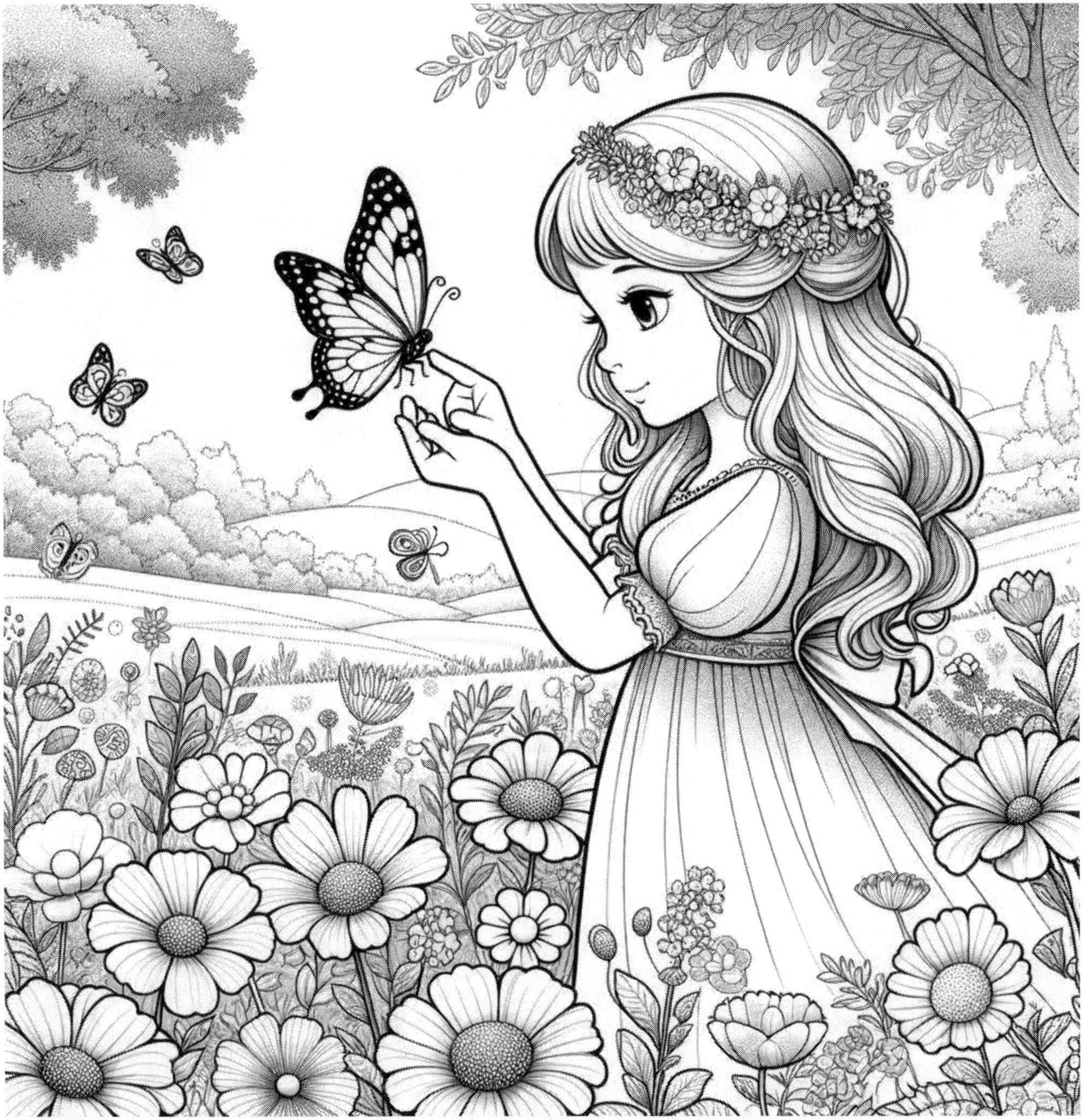

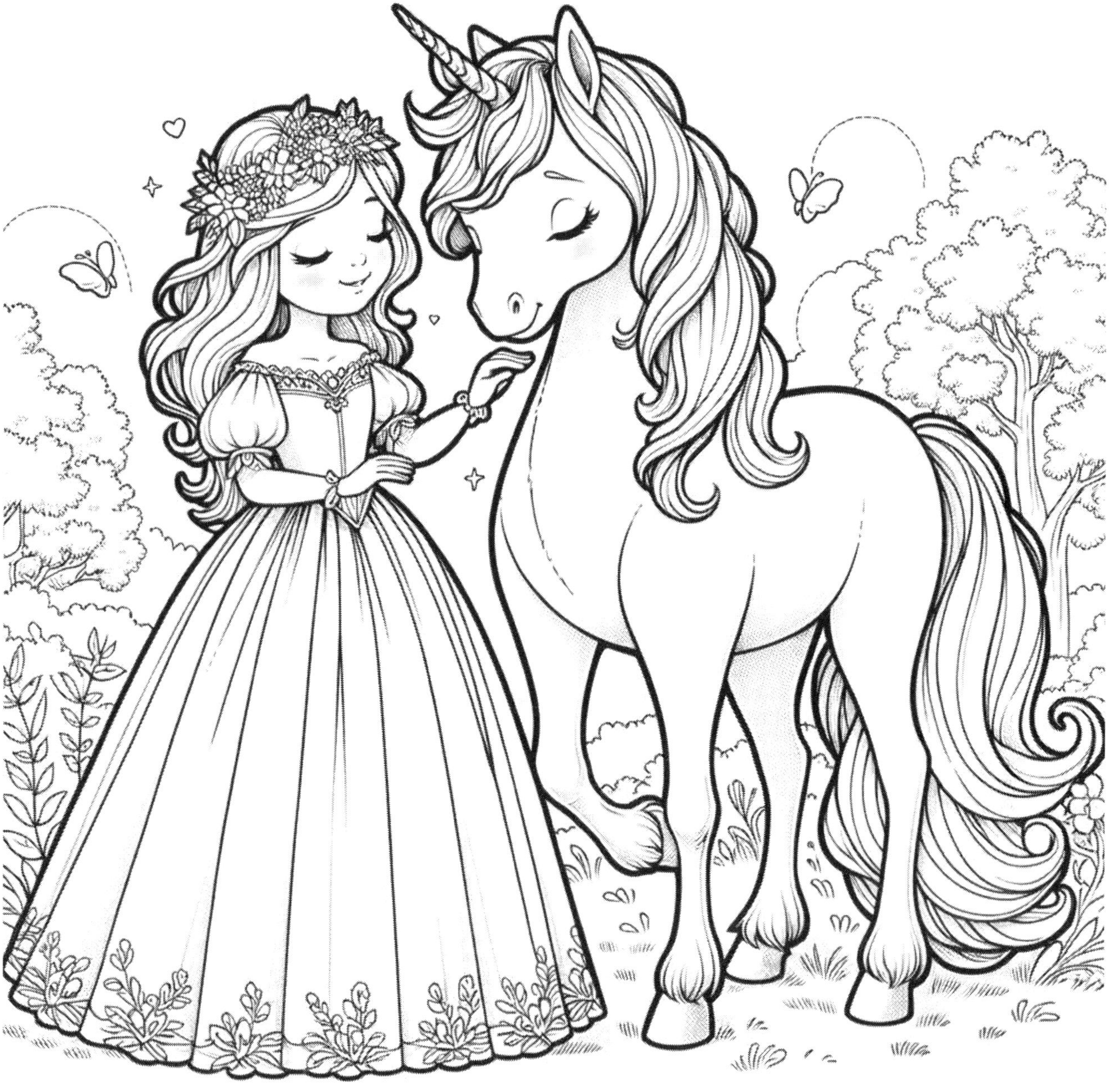

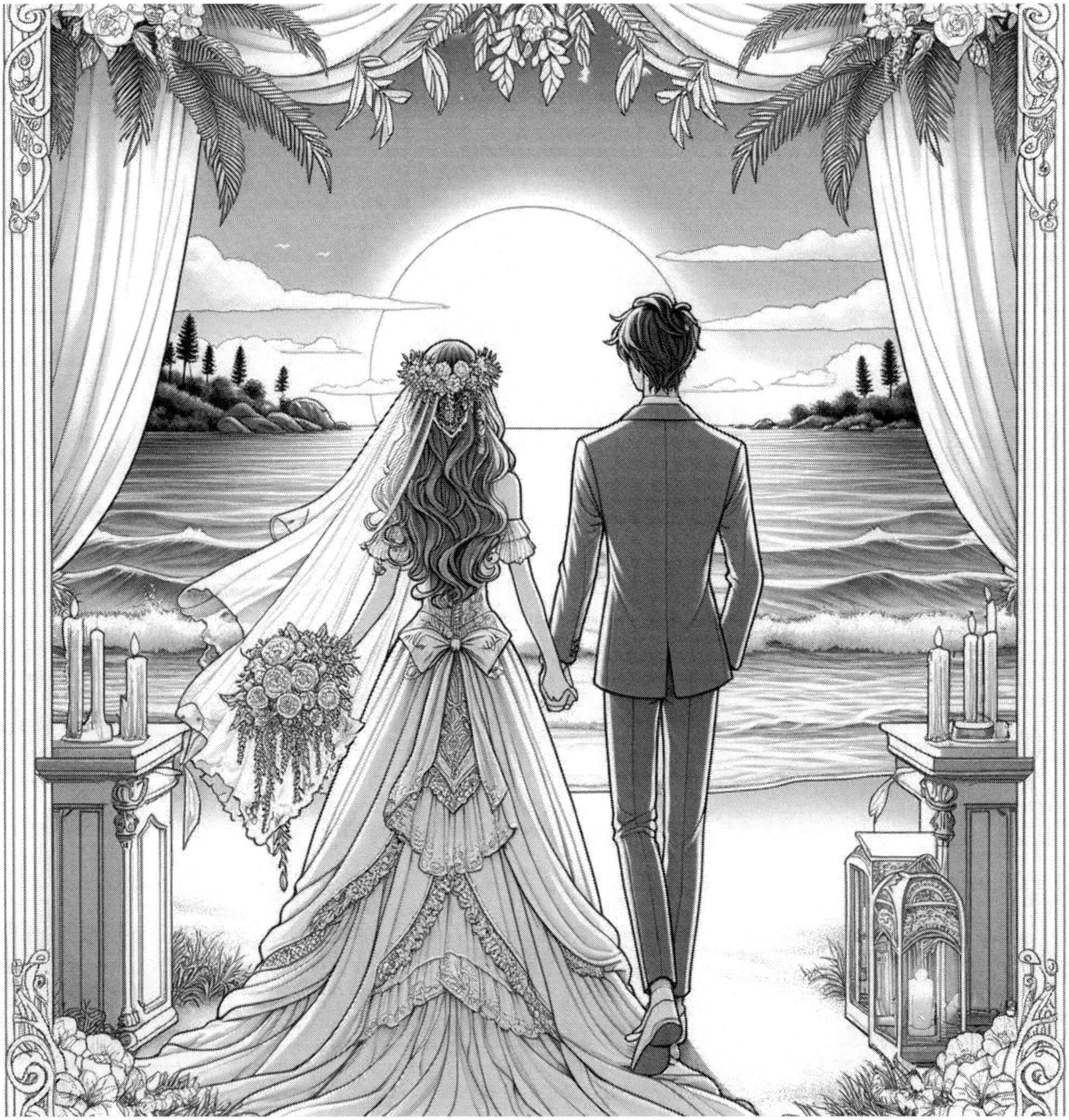

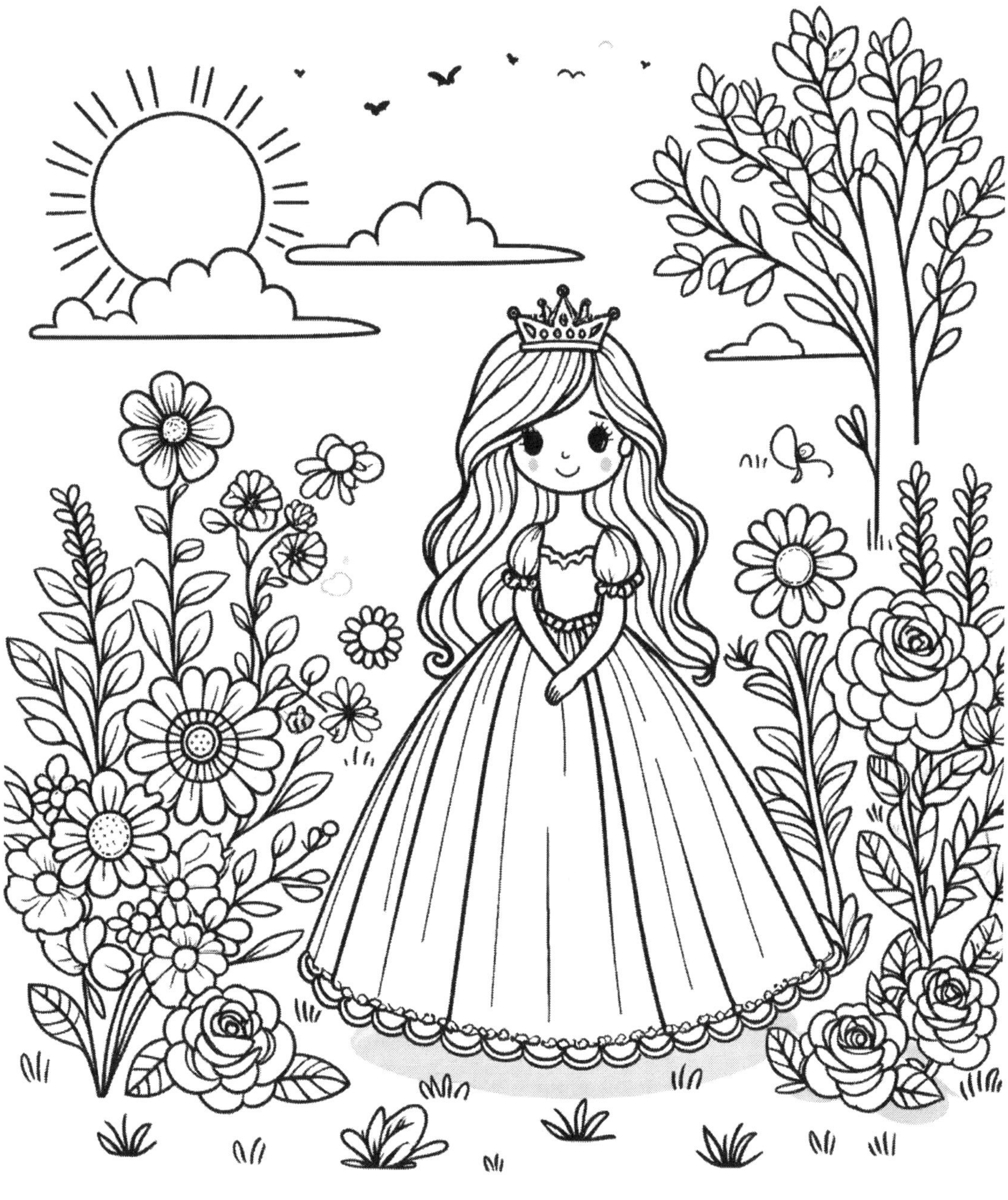

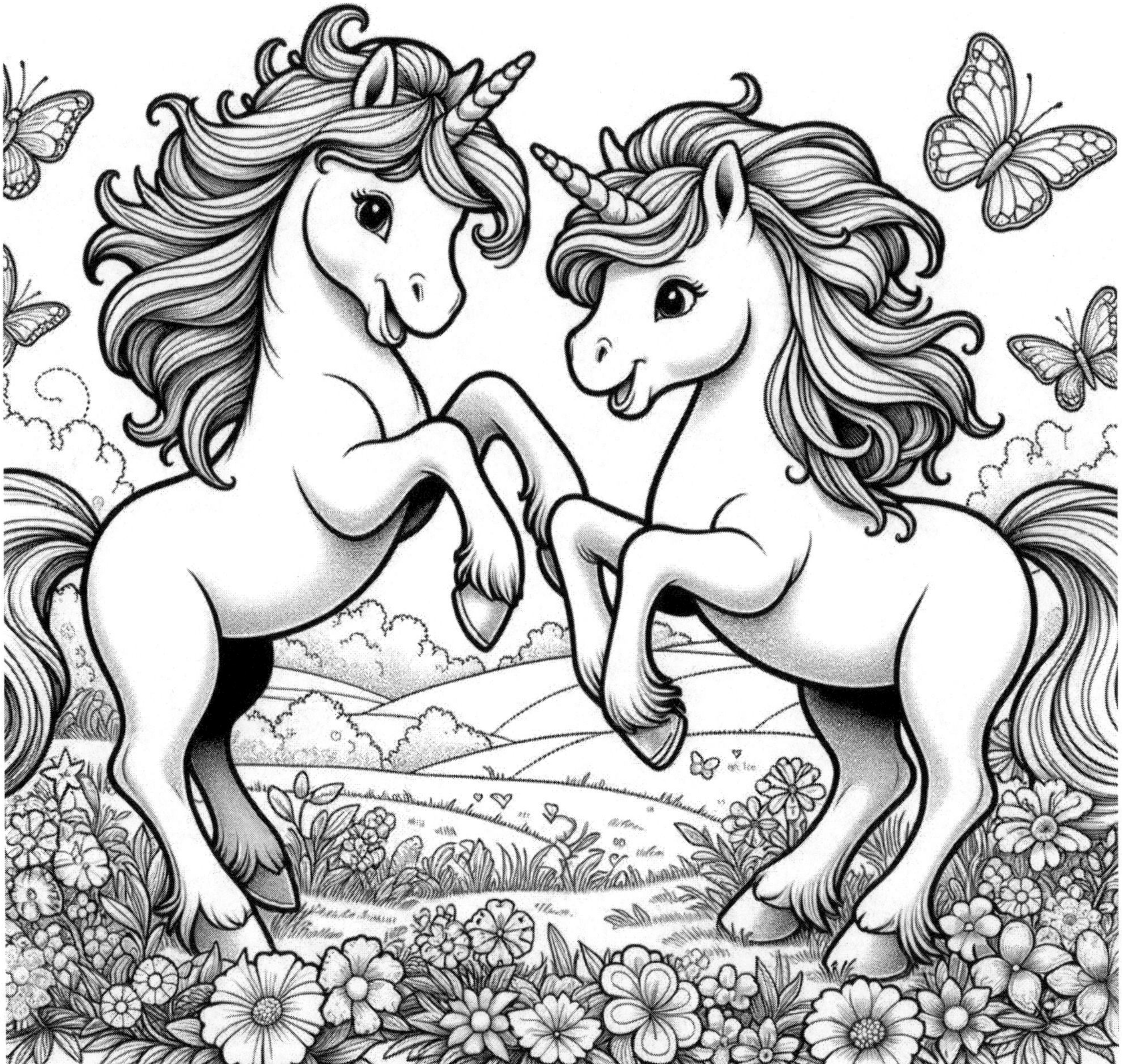

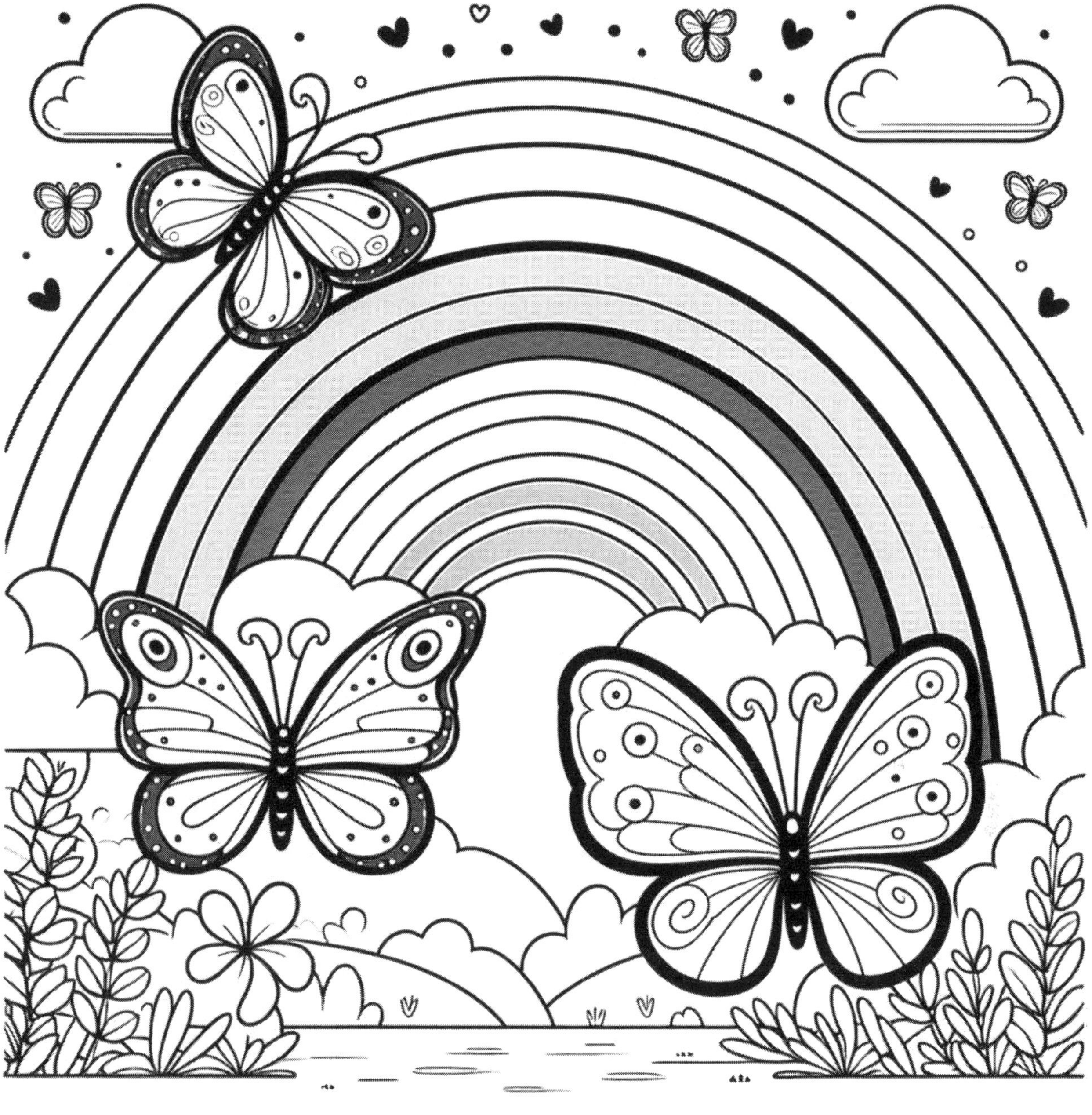

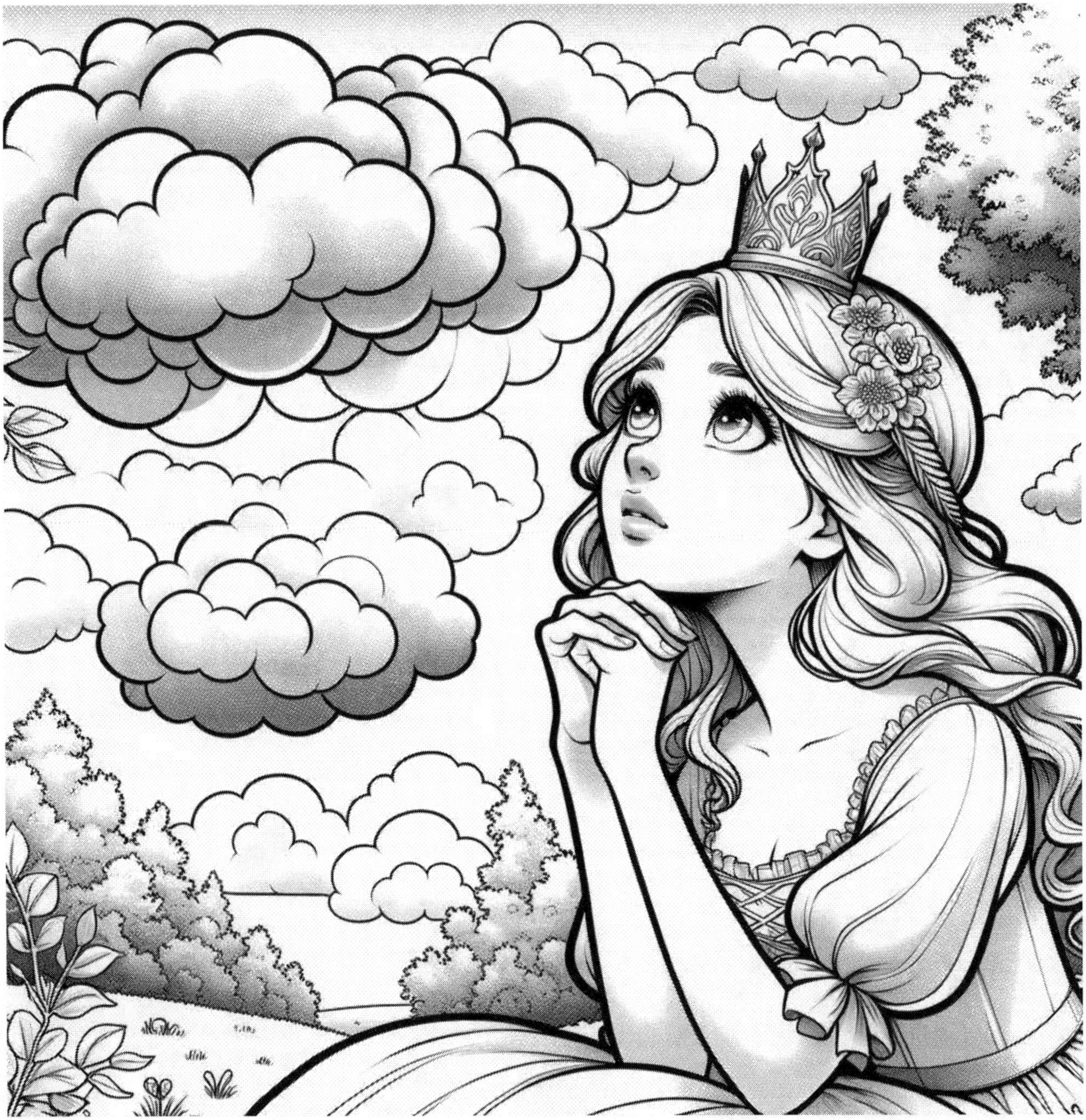

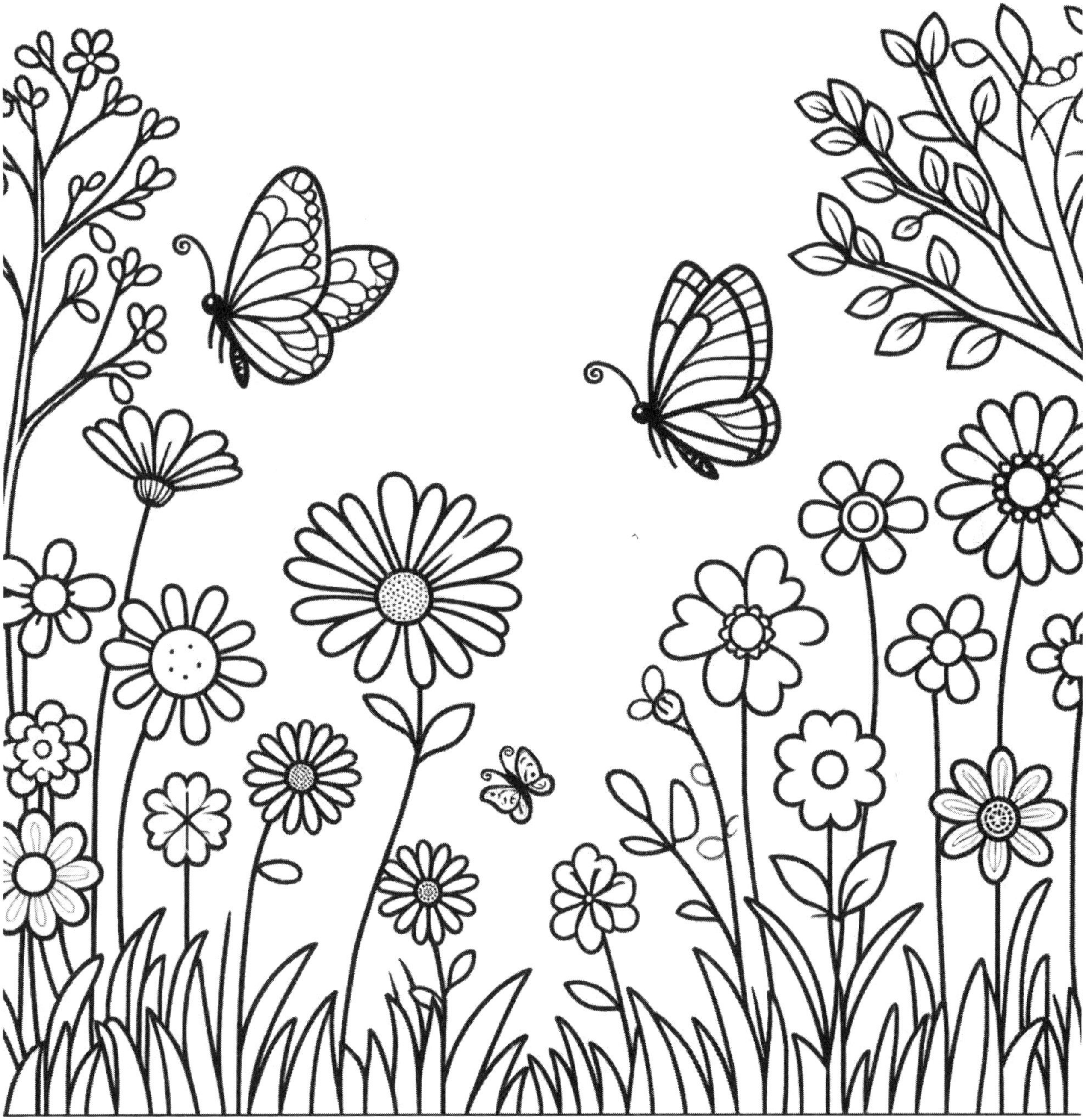

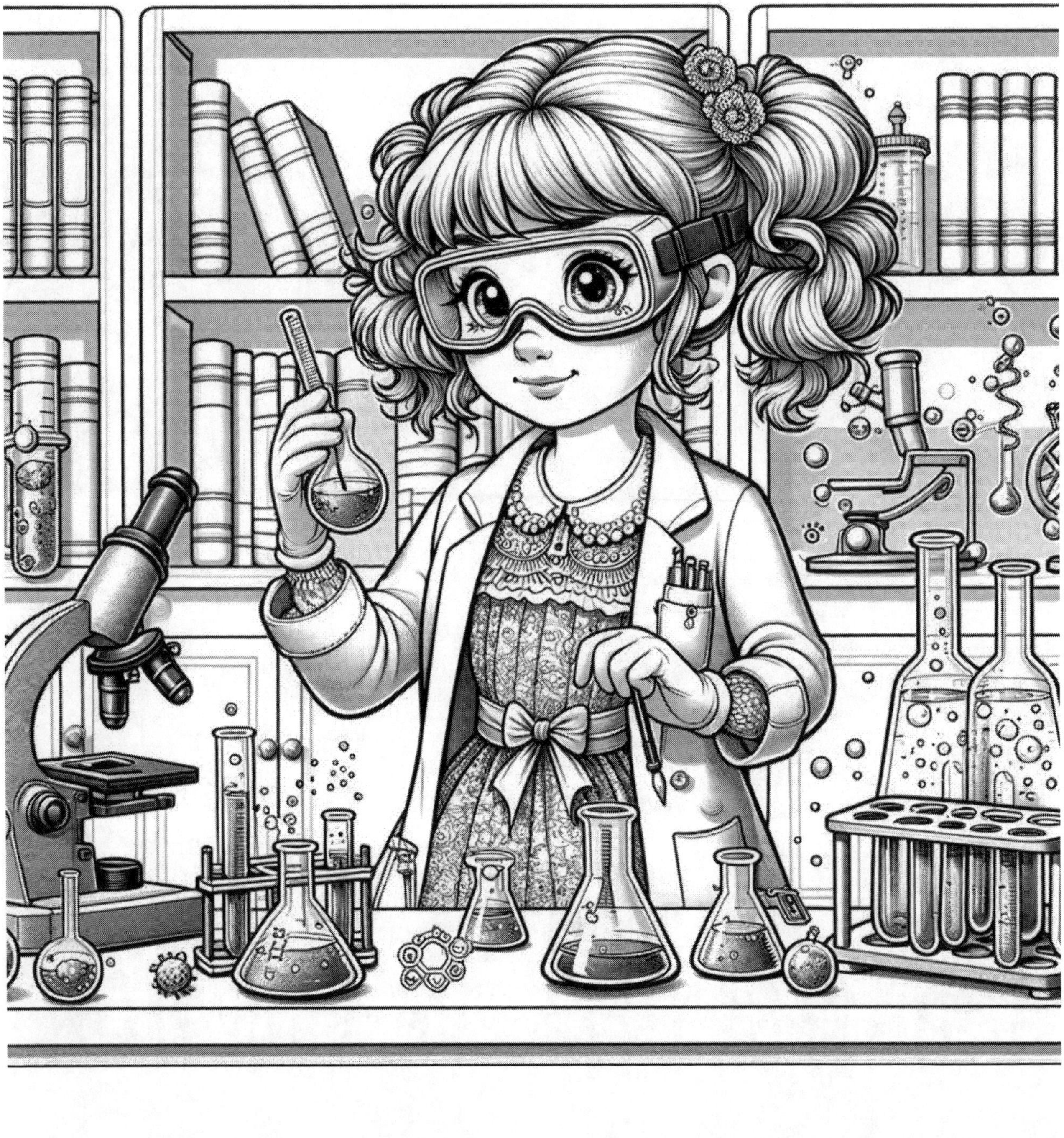

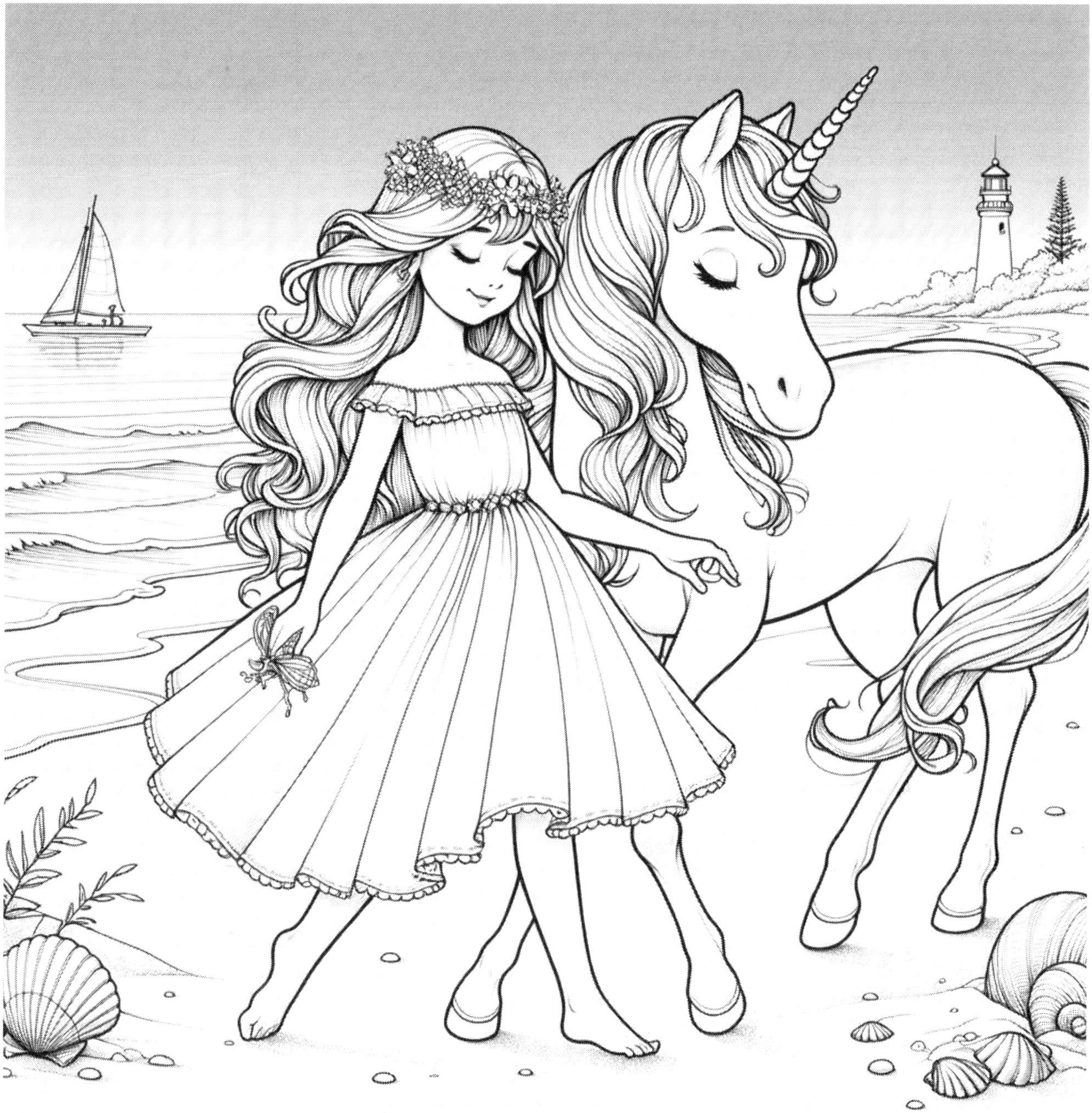

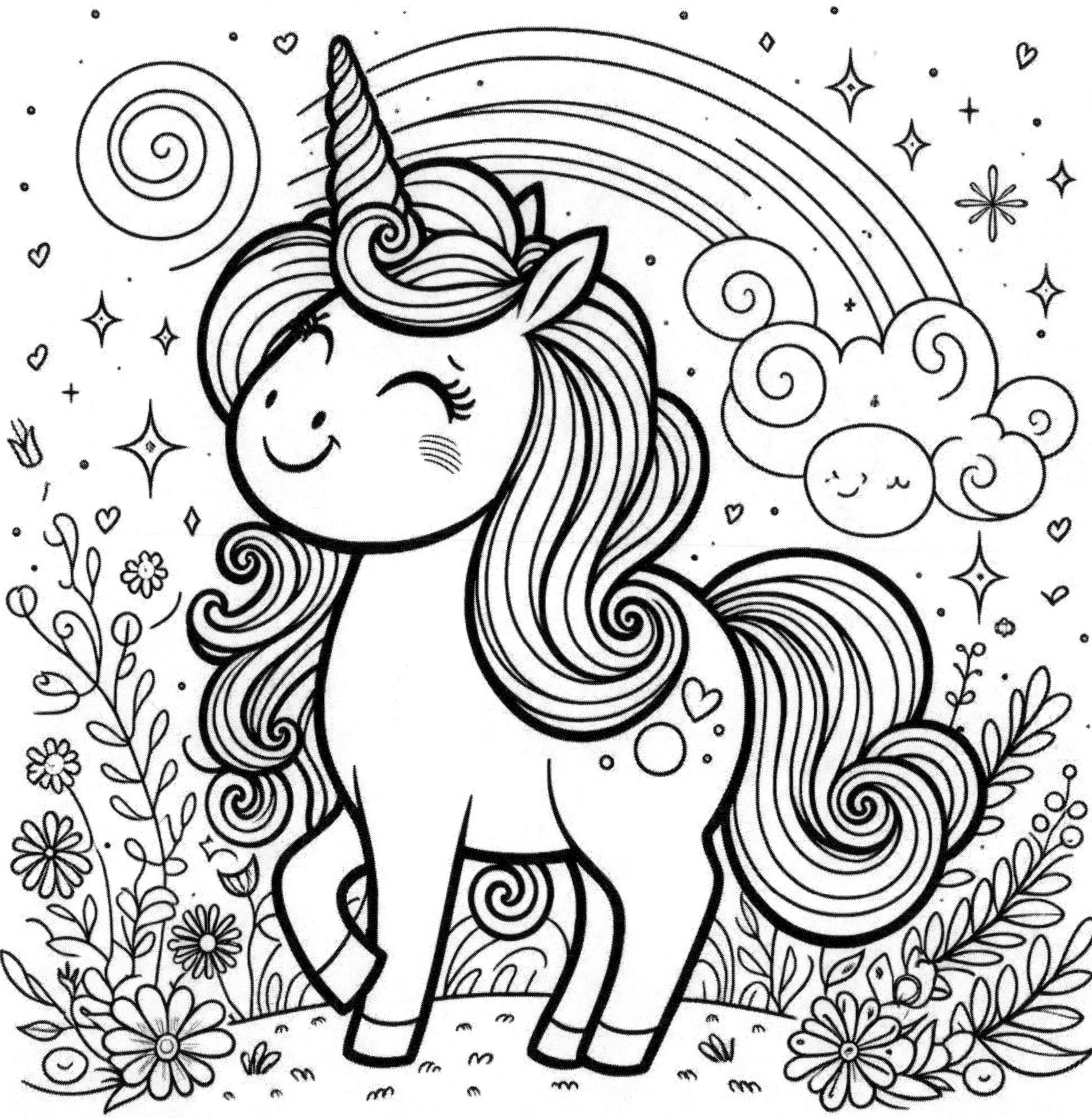

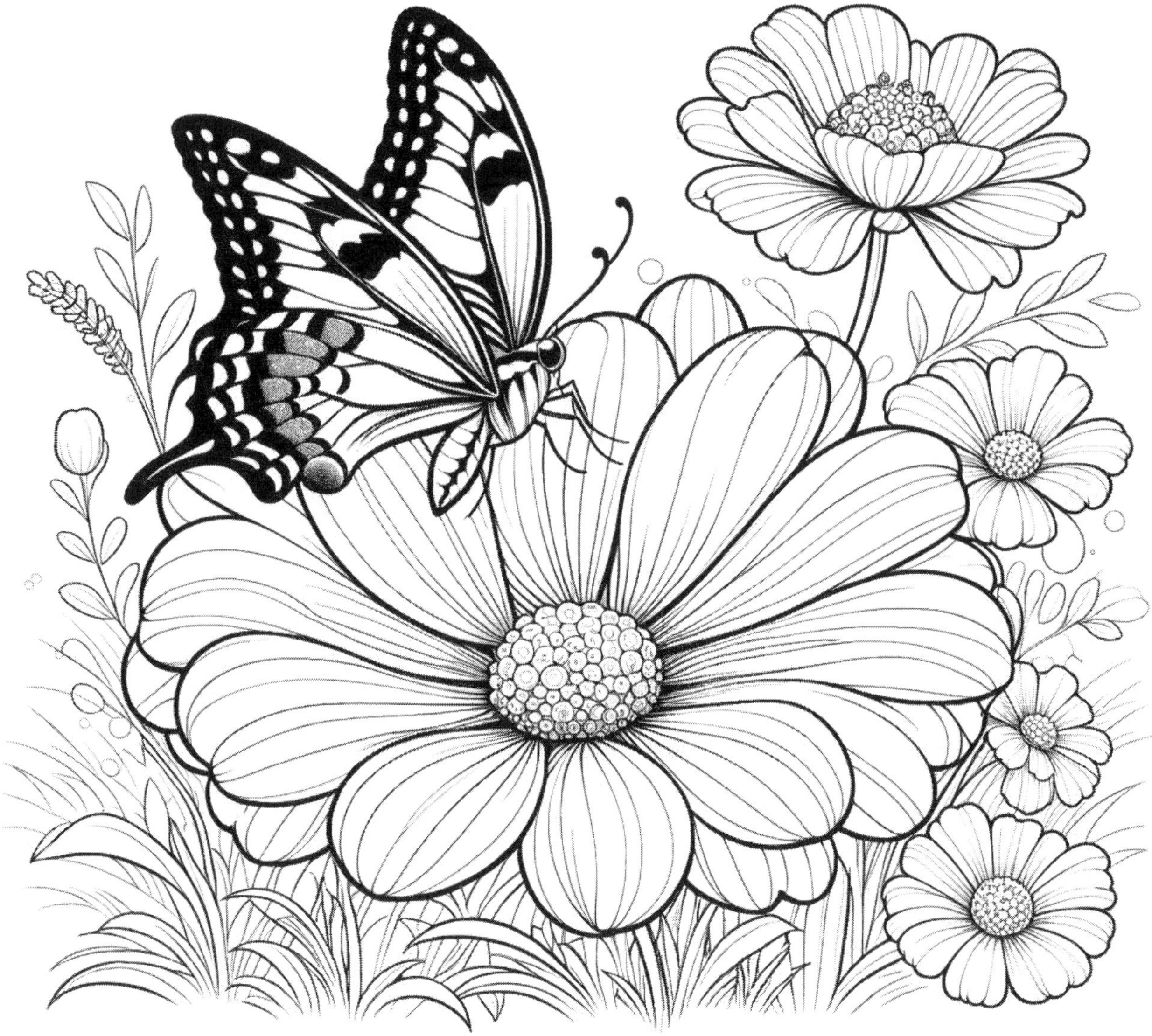

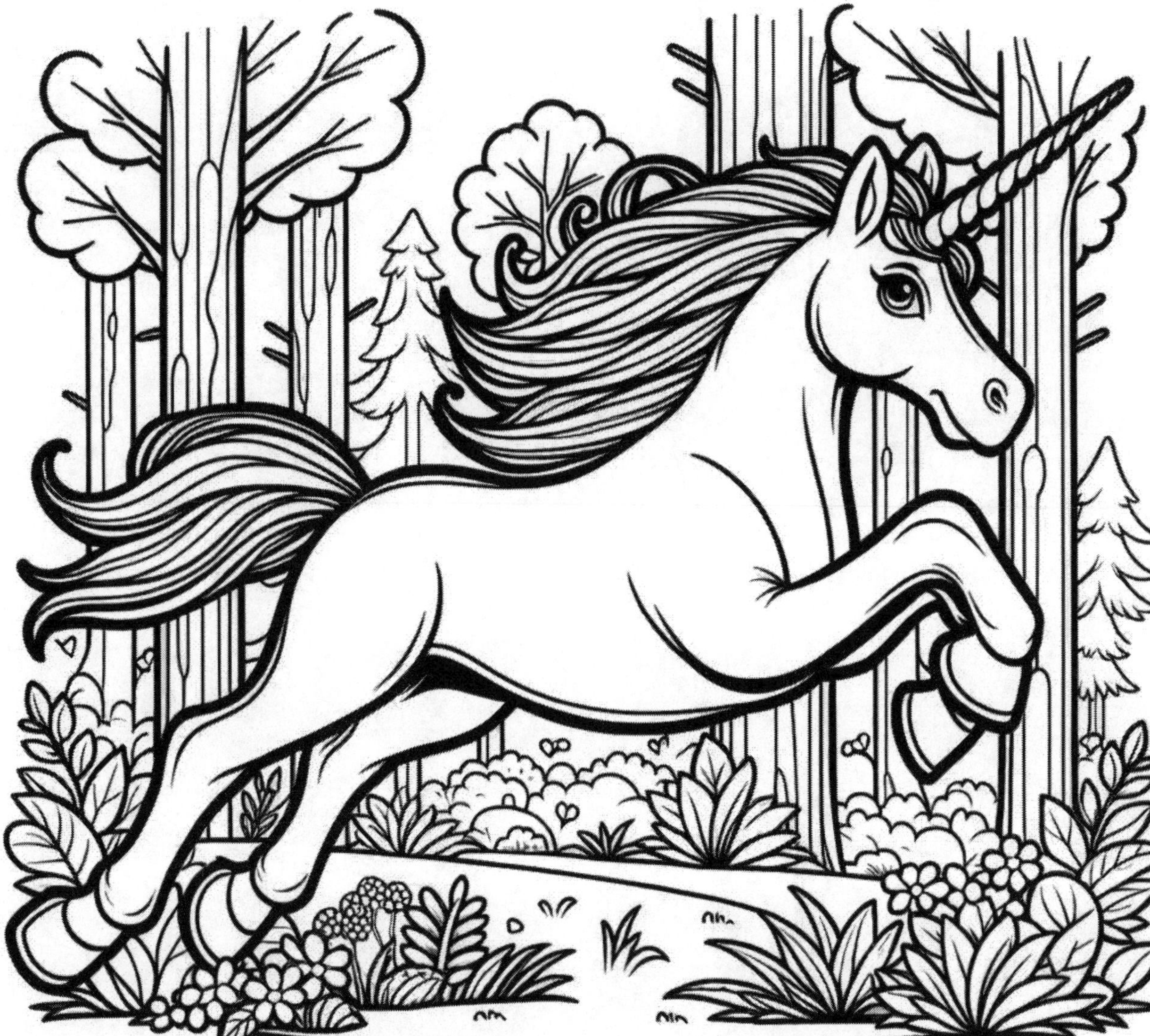

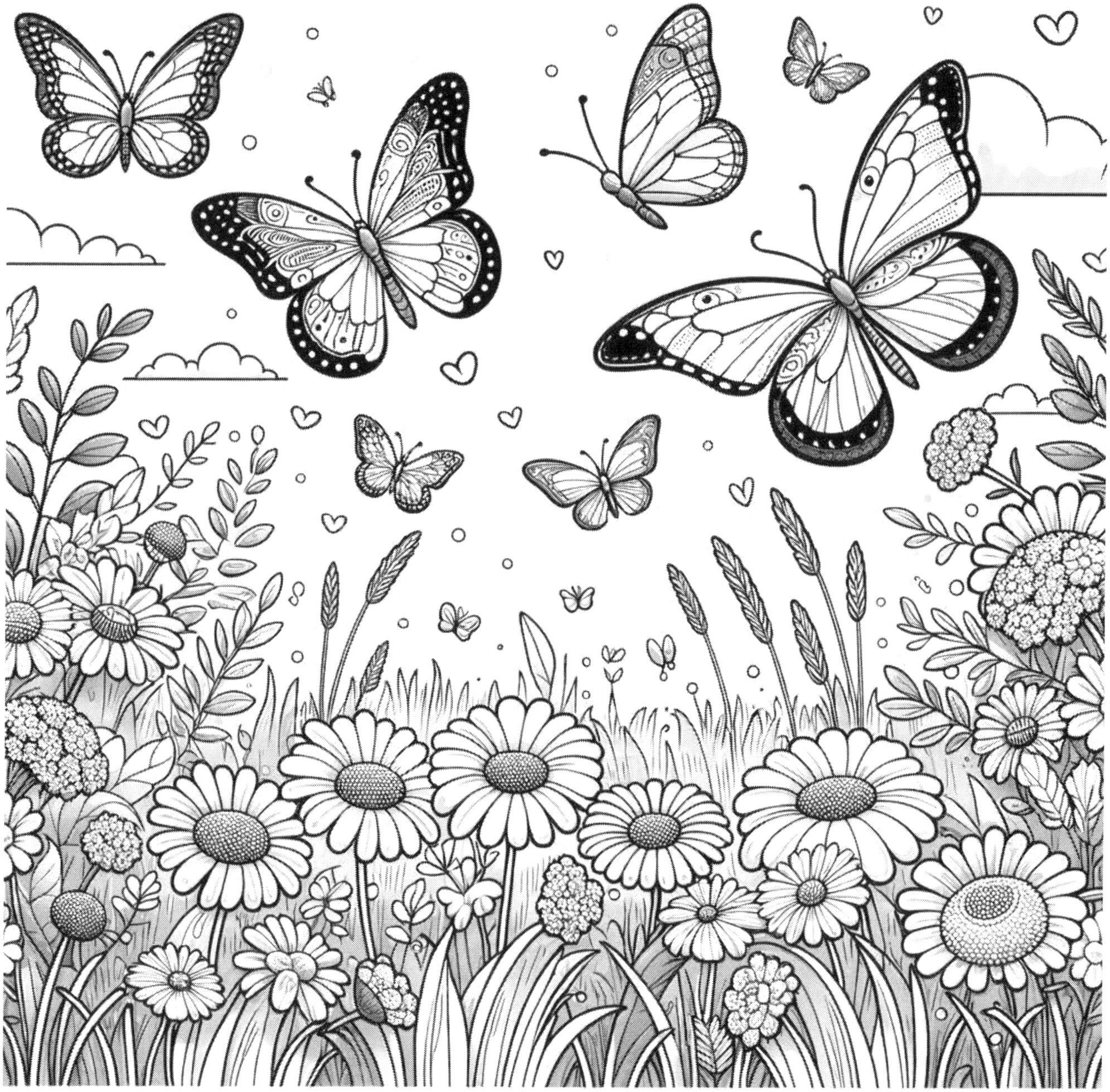

Made in United States
Troutdale, OR
12/17/2024

26776752R00029